I Am I

I Am I

'From The Light Of Wisdom'

108 Messages from the Heart

Saraswathi Ma

BALBOA
PRESS

A DIVISION OF HAY HOUSE

Balboa Press books may be ordered through booksellers or by contacting:
Balboa Press
A Division of Hay House
1663 Liberty Drive
Bloomington, IN 47403
www.balboapress.com
1 (877) 407-4847

Printed in the United States of America.

ISBN: 978-1-4525-1920-3 (sc)
ISBN: 978-1-4525-1921-0 (e)

Balboa Press rev. date: 08/15/2014

For, through, and by the Grace of His
Holiness Sri Sathya Sai Baba

For all

This is your *Real* estate. Your true Home.

one

I AM HERE. You never have to look anywhere, for I am here. Not even in your heart, for I am your heart. There is nothing to fear, but fear will come. Fear will come to wash you out of you, to remind you who you are. How auspicious is this moment! The fruit has ripened, sweet and succulent. The spotlight has turned itself inward, so that you may see that I am your own Self. For a long time now you have been looking for Me externally. All is well. All beings must first look outwards, so as eventually to turn around. And what an exquisite journey it has been, playing its part just as I willed it, so that you would come to see there is only I.

What is this I? This is the question that shall light a fire in your soul and return you to I. It is so intimate your mind will tremble. But all is well. The mind is held while it trembles. Like a baby in its mother's arms, it is held when it cries. So, let fear come, let pain be felt, let all unfold as it must. You are Love in form. Even if you don't yet know this to be the Reality, dive into Love wherever you hear it singing. For each

1

being Love sings its unique love-song; in a field, in a church, in a teacher. Go there; bathe there; for in bathing you are talking with Me. Every day, every moment we are talking. You do not need to find a quiet place to talk with Love. Your own Silence is eternally quiet. You have been born to know Silence, to know Love, to know I. The only thing that is required is everything. Throw everything at My feet. Put yourself like a baby in My arms. Be as that baby who is not trying to know anything. Then you shall know Freedom. For in not knowing, in handing over all your concepts, you shall live. You shall swim in the Ocean of Existence and all happenings shall unfold in your unending Awareness.

There is nothing to fear. Though fear will come. Fear will dig deep into your psyche and help you unearth everything that has kept you bound in your personality. Be prepared to lay everything under the microscope. Be prepared for scrutiny. Be willing to hand yourself over to Love's scrutiny. Do not seek to be *with* Love. You *are* Love in expression; you are Consciousness in form. Only we must peel back those layers so that this form which comprises the individual you may shine fully in the Light of You.

two

*L*OVE TAKES form to show you the Love that you are, which means to take you beyond need. The human story is to chase a need of love without realising that what is being chased is right here as our own Self. And yet, there is wisdom to the chase. Somewhere deep within there is an inexplicable knowing that happiness lies in love, that completion lies in love. At the same time, there is a deep dissatisfaction, for the love that is found in the world, no matter how beautiful, is never enough. There remains a sense that a deeper completion is needed.

The need for love contains both wisdom and misunderstanding. The wisdom lies in the recognition that happiness *does* lie in love; the misunderstanding is the need to look outwards for an external form. So, why do we look outwards, why are humans so filled with need? The moment a human being is confirmed as a person—the moment he or she receives their name—a feeling of isolation and loneliness begins. Somewhere deep within the person is an un-nameable feeling, akin perhaps to a profound sense of homesickness. And in that 'homesickness', without having any clear idea yet where that home might be, the person feels that something must be missing and that therefore something must be sought. Where there is a sense of lack there is need, and this need to 'fill the gap' is the driving force of every human impetus. Although it is not in the beginning clear what this home might look like, there is a knowing within—like a far distant remembrance of a former way—that directs the human being on a very singular trajectory. It is as if he or she were chasing a voice that is calling to them from the deep recesses of the heart. And so the human being sets off on a journey that must take them into the great labyrinth of life.

The deep-rooted feeling that happiness somehow lies in love leads human beings into the greatest search that ever was born—the search for Love. Every possible path will be taken—in relationship, in work, in pursuit—in the search for that which feels absent. That mysterious and magnetic voice sings from what feels like the far-off distance. In the beginning of the search the capacity to listen is still developing, and so the actual proximity of that voice is not yet realised. But all is just as it should be. A worldly search must unfold, creating and compounding for a time dense layers of misunderstanding. Each being's story has its own plotline of misunderstanding and need. Each being's world view is built upon personal experiences and reactions to those experiences. From the very first experience of parental love, which itself shall have its psychological roots in need, our personal understanding of love and our need of it becomes fixed in the psyche. When we do not receive what we feel we need we suffer. And so we build

4

walls in self-defence, walls of greater need. How to knock down these walls? First is the recognition that something *is* missing. Remembrance of your true nature is missing—you have forgotten the Love that you are. So, how to know the Love that you are? Use wherever you are to begin an enquiry. And ask: *who am I?*

What is this I that I am?

✤ three ✤

I CAN HEAR birdsong outside of the window. I am aware that I can hear notes and trills, and now a faint cawing over the top. These sounds are clear and distinct in my hearing. I tune in to the noises themselves, and feel my focus going inward. Then a question comes: I know that I am listening, but who is this I that is aware of the hearing of sounds? I pull my attention into this I, into the me that is aware. I try to find this I.

Immediately, a sneeze comes. It pulls the body this way and that, it pulls the attention towards its noise and the body sensations it creates. Outwardly, it may appear to disturb the peace of the moment. But does it disturb the I that is aware of the sneeze? I look and see. I turn my focus, as if it were a torch, inside. I tune in to this me that is aware of the sneeze. What can I say about this me? I cannot touch this me that is aware. I cannot see this me. This me is not limited to the boundary of my body. It feels expansive, as if it had no edges, like space. It has no shape, no form, nothing tangible that can be seen. It simply is.

So, is this Is-ness *doing* anything; did the me that is aware sneeze? The answer eats me alive, for the most I can say is that this me is simply watching; it is *aware*. It is the one who is watching the sneeze without itself sneezing. It is Awareness itself. Awareness-I is the formless-I, the one who is watching a little I sneeze. So, does that mean I am watching every aspect of I? Does that mean I am watching the me who looks, who listens, who breathes, who speaks, who tastes, who likes, who dislikes, who *thinks?*

❧ four ❧

I T IS SO. You are the eternal thought-watcher. The mind is a hive of thought-activity. But don't worry about how many thoughts are coming. If the mind is busy let it be so. It is not up to you to rush and sort these thoughts out—not just yet. Examination can come in due course. You have spent many years believing in your thoughts, believing yourself to *be* your thoughts. So, the first step is to begin to separate yourself from them.

You know that you exist. If there were one thing that you could say that you know, would it not be that you exist? Only, can you with pure knowing say what you *exist as*? Can you in this moment draw your attention to your *sense of Existence*, that innate sense of *Being*? Not 'I am a woman' or 'I am a man'; simply, I am. Can you touch your sense of Being, your sense of I-Am-ness? Is it a form, is it visible, is it male or female? The deeper your focus on that sense of Being, the more it is seen that your sense of Being has no shape, no form, no limit, no sex, no distinction other than *space* that is somehow watching.

Was this not your exact description of Awareness? Your own enquiry shall reveal that your innate sense of Existence is synonymous with Awareness itself. You know you exist; and now you are coming to see that what you exist *as* is formless, shapeless, limitless Awareness.

So, having drawn your attention to your sense of Awareness-Being, now you may watch your thoughts. See how many come. Observe: how long do they stay? And how many thoughts do you have in a minute? You may discover there to be hundreds. In one minute alone your mind can entertain so many thoughts that you lose count. Pinpoint one thought. Let us say that your thought is that you are hungry. Can you hold on to this thought? Almost immediately another arrives—you are hungry but don't know what to eat. Then another—you need to go shopping; then another—you won't have time today because you have to work late; then another— this exercise is silly; then another—the film last night was fantastic; then another—a feeling of anxiety at having to go into work ... And all of those thoughts in a matter of seconds perhaps. And all the time your attention runs to them. But who are you who is *aware* of these thoughts? Who are you who is aware of the attention being pulled?

By observing your thoughts, you see that they come and go. They do not stay for long—particular ones may return to bite you, but even the most tenacious are never permanently there. So, if your thoughts are not permanently there, you may ask is *anything* permanently there? Look close and discover. Does Awareness change, does it leave, does it move, does it hop to 'another awareness'? No, your own seeing shall reveal that Awareness is ever so, ever silent, ever there; non-moving and unchanging. In that case, who is the *essential* you? Are you the thoughts that come and go, or are you that which is permanently aware of your thoughts? For this moment, reside in that sense of Awareness-Being and ask yourself: who am I? Am I fundamentally the thoughts that change? Or am I the Awareness that is ever present?

five

ALREADY YOU don't know. What a beautiful place to be in. From here the wide canvas of Existence is seen. Not to know is to dance; is to be free. You have been struggling to know for so long, and in this instant all struggle is seen to be what it is: but a means to discover who you are. Which is why, always be thankful for whatever Life sends. Can you begin to see the benevolence of Life? That it gives in order to teach, that it gives in order to free you. There is no such thing as 'bad', there is only misunderstanding. Misunderstanding keeps you away from your Self. It keeps you looking outwards, like a child endlessly seeking new toys. You are ready to receive the greatest gift of all—Self-recognition. Only you must trust Me; you must have faith. Many beings do not realise their innate beauty, their innate wisdom. To come to this realisation, they first have to have faith in what they initially perceive to be another. In time, this perception will turn in on itself and reveal that there is no 'other'. But for now, look to Me in whatever form pleases your heart and hand yourself to Me. This surrender is the kindest, most severe form of love. That is to say, it will undo you. It will decapitate this you you think yourself to be and reveal what you have always been, all along.

Every child must take its first step. It is a step inward that reveals your true parent, your own Self. Trust the Mother, for She is loving you endlessly, tirelessly, guiding you Home. No matter what may unfold, know that it is for your benefit, always.

❧ six ❧

WHERE AM I physically right now? I am on the sofa.
I am sat cross-legged, the weight of the dog's head
pressing on my thigh. My arms have to stretch over him to
reach the keyboard. I also feel the heat of the cat beside me. I
hear the ticking of the clock. There is the sound of a woman
singing. There is the faint sound of birdsong behind all that.
There is the sensation of cool air in my nostrils, coming in
from the open window. I can feel the air in my eyes. I can
taste the leftover flavour of chamomile tea in my mouth.
My eyes are scratchy. I am thinking maybe it is pollen, or
perhaps dust. The voice changes in the woman's song and my
attention is drawn to that. My ears are burning inside. There
is slight tension in my stomach. I feel the muscles of my back
against the sofa. I feel the ache in my muscles from yesterday's
walk. I rub my eye hard and see blue spots in front of my
vision. I hear my lungs take a large in-breath. I yawn. My
nose is running, my eyes are itching. I feel my chest tighten.
A thought comes that some allergic reaction is taking place.

I notice my breathing has shortened. Then my attention is pulled to my thirst.

Where am *I*? Am I my thirst? Am I my listening? Am I the one who is sensing my muscles? Am I the one yawning, feeling the yawn, hearing the yawn; am I the one feeling the air, hearing the clock, tasting the tea, feeling the heavy weight of the dog's head on my lap; am I the nose that runs or the eyes that itch; am I the sensations that occur in both and the actions that follow both? Am I the body that is sat on the sofa? Am I the attention that keeps jumping from one experience to another? How many I's am I?

Who is aware of this attention that can move from one experience to another? Who is aware of the listening that is happening? Who is aware of all these sensations and feelings and thoughts arising in this moment? I am. I am aware of the listening, the tasting, the smelling, the thinking, the sensing. I am aware of all this movement. I am even aware of my attention that moves. So, who is this I who is aware? I cannot locate this I. It is not sat on the sofa, but my body is there within I. I cannot touch, smell or hear this I. I draw my focus into this I. I discover that this I is my awareness. I am my awareness. I cannot even say 'my awareness', for I *am* Awareness. I cannot possess what I am. All of this body/mind activity occurs within I. I am not having an allergic reaction, but an allergic reaction is occurring within I. I am beyond. I am like a vast silence. I *am* Silence, prior to and containing all experience. Silence, Awareness, Beingness, Existence, Self, Truth: this is the Consciousness of I.

✦ seven ✦

FROM THE moment you open your eyes in the morning until the moment you sleep at night you are guided by the flow of your thinking process. Countless thoughts in the form of sensations, memories, feelings, hopes, plans, desires and ideas have formed the framework of your existence. Thoughts have been so personal to you that you cannot separate yourself from them, or imagine life without them. It feels as if life *is* thought.

Dependence on thoughts is born out of thought—a belief that 'I am separate from you'. From this root thought comes all the misunderstanding that you see in this world. Misunderstanding can be brought to understanding not by trying to stop thought, but by becoming the *observer* of thought. This observer is Wisdom itself. So, see once again if you can bring your attention to the I that is watching all movement in your mind. We say '*my* thoughts', which suggests already that there is something there to which the thoughts belong. Who is this me who is witnessing its own thoughts? Is this me itself thinking? Or is it merely the silent observer to all movement within the mind? Can you find this you who is watching you? What is the quality of the watching you?

The me that is watching has no physical form that I can see or touch. It is a no-thing-ness, like space. The more I rest as the space that I am, the deeper I feel the compassion that I am. I am a vast peace that never ends. This is the Love that I have been searching for throughout lifetimes. I know it without knowing how I know it, and that is how I know it to be true. This is what I have been aching to find; this is why I have felt so homesick. *I* am the Love that has no edges. *I* am the Love that encompasses everything. There is no separation when I look from Love. This is the quality of I.

eight

I F SOMEONE were to ask you who you are, it seems so simple and obvious to reply. This is my name. I am the son/daughter of these people; I was born here, educated there; this is what I like, this is what I don't like; these are my friends, these are my beliefs, my hopes and my dreams; this is where I live now, this is where I would like to live in the future; these are my memories, these are the experiences I have had, these are the people I have loved. You think this comprises you, contains you, describes you, *is* you. Your personality feels the summation of you. But somewhere that you cannot locate there is a feeling of discontentment, of sadness, of loneliness, of incompleteness, a feeling that something is missing. Even if you have everything that you think your heart desires, there is still some outward longing. But for what, you cannot be sure. For as long as you cannot be sure what this *something* is, you will keep on searching outwardly for material things to fill that gap, for relationships to fill that gap, for personal success to fill that gap. Only once you stop the outward search and turn the spotlight inward will it be seen that that which you felt yourself to be searching for outwardly, was none other than your own Self.

This does not mean your personality-self. So, what *does* it mean? This is your discovery to discover, your treasure to unlock. It is the nature of your own existence. It is to understand the real nature of You. This you who you think yourself to be is an appearance *within* You. What happens if you draw your attention to that sense of Being? Reside there, simply in that sense of being alive. Can you touch this sense? Does your sense of Existence have a discernible shape? Is it male or female? Is it *doing* anything? A doubt may come. Let it voice itself, and then pull yourself back into that sense of your Being. Throw your inner spotlight on the space of your Being that is *aware* of the doubt and ask: is Awareness-Being doing anything, feeling anything? Thoughts will come, let them. Feelings will come, let them. Emotions will come, let them. Your only responsibility in this moment is to focus your attention on your sense of Existence.

What is your discovery? Is anything missing?

✦ nine ✦

THE BODY and mind are ready to be capsized; in fact, they themselves may be used to capsize themselves! Each body/mind is a unique instrument for remembering You. What a paradox that through it you shall come to see that you are beyond it. The mind can be an unruly, wilful monkey, and will cause distraction at every opportunity. But, this monkey is also your gift, for it is through its play that you will come to know You. So, the minute you feel its unruliness, put your left hand on the centre of your chest. Allow your focus to settle on the touch between hand and chest. The mind is so active that even this simple act of concentration can be a challenge. But the more you concentrate on the touch, the more you will feel your focus move inward.

Now see if you can deepen your focus. See if you can feel the *space* between hand and chest. Drop down into this vibration, into the space of your being, and feel your own energetic presence—the you that is not your body, but is still *you*. This we can call the *heart* of you. Ask yourself: is the space of your being—is the heart of you—limited to between hand and chest, or does it somehow go beyond? Sink into the expansiveness of space, and see if you can find a limit to space; see if you can find a limit to *You*. This is what it means to be capsized, for notice the quality of the body/mind when your focus is here in the heart-space of You.

If anxiety comes, drop your focus to the heart; if distraction comes, drop down to the heart; if anger comes, drop down to the heart; if confusion or fear come, drop down to the heart; if feelings of happiness, excitement, courage or joy come—at any moment, in all moments—drop down to the *heart*. How does it feel when you look from here? Look as if you were looking from a pair of eyes in the centre of your chest. How is your view from these deeper eyes? Is anything missing?

❦ ten ❧

ALL HUMAN beings are in fear until they realise they are not separate from 'other things'. Fear is so rooted in our personalities that we do not even know it is there. The mind thinks, I am this person and you are that person. Immediately, there is isolation; there is difference, and a belief that 'I am separate from you'. This difference brings fear; it brings the unconscious need to protect ourselves from all 'difference'. An idea of separation brings with it a feeling of loneliness. This loneliness is not just a feeling; it is the thinking base of all our movements. Because we consider ourselves to be first and foremost a person, we cannot help but feel continuously isolated, separate and alone, continuously in a state of fear for our welfare. The one who is identified as being a person has therefore two objectives in mind: first, to seek its own protection, and second, to seek love from another person in order to fill this apparent well of loneliness.

How do we break from this cage? As long as we are

dependent on thoughts we remain trapped. As long as we believe ourselves to *be* our thoughts we remain trapped. As long as we plunge into each emotion that comes along, believing ourselves to *be* the emotion, we remain trapped. Imagine they were someone else's thoughts, someone else's emotions. If a friend were to share their feelings with you, you would be able to speak and give comfort from a compassionate distance because you would not feel swamped by the emotion. You do not feel swamped because you can say to yourself: they are not my thoughts, so therefore I am not attached to them. So how to cultivate a meaningful distance so that you may watch your every thought, sensation, idea and emotion without judgement? How to be as the loving witness so that you may watch from compassionate Silence itself?

Begin by placing your left hand on the centre of your chest. We can use the body to take you beyond your body. We can use it as a point of concentration. So, it may be easier to close your eyes. Settle your focus on the touch there, hand to chest. Allow yourself to sink into the sensation. See how the muscles of your body soften when you focus directly on this touch; even the mind softens. Allow your focus to go inward, inside you; inside the *space* of you. Melt into this space; into the space of your being. Notice how everything softens even more; how space spreads beyond hand and chest; how it cannot be contained. See if you can find a limit to this space of Being.

Notice the quality of space—like a vast stillness; a vast silence. The silence of You, the silence of your Awareness, is the Silence that is watching everything; is aware of everything. It is watching you breathe. It is watching you listen. It is watching you touch. It is watching you think. You as Awareness are watching the little you. Now you are discovering the You that is beyond all form; the limitless You that contains all form. How does it feel to watch from here, to watch *as* Silence, as Stillness, as the Peace that you are?

✺ eleven ✺

A THOUGHT is merely an arising in Consciousness; it is not the enemy. From the expansive view of I any thought can come. But its substance will be different. Such an arising will not be loaded with previous experience; it will be fresh and uncluttered by emotional memory. Such 'thoughts' are beyond the identified personal position. They come not in reaction, not out of any thinking process as such; but as a spontaneous expression of Love. We could then call them *thoughtless thoughts*.

Identified thoughts have been forming your entire view. You are looking at the world through a personal filter. Every experience and every reaction to experience is adding to your filter. All the details of your story are providing your filter; in other words, your understanding of the world is based on everything that has happened to you throughout the course of your life. Such a perspective is necessarily limited. And it is not only the experiences that cause your coloured view, but the personal perspective you have had on your own experiences.

If, for example, four siblings all experience the loss of a parent, each of the four will have their own unique reaction to the same experience. This reaction is, we might say, their personalised script of emotional wiring. Each child has come into the world with its own set of tendencies, its own way of looking at things. And each new happening along the way compounds and develops this way of looking at things. It is so intimate to the child that even as it grows into adulthood, it cannot perceive that someone else does not see things in the same way. The child growing into adulthood feels ever more isolated, for it feels unable to make anyone see things the way it sees them. It feels therefore in a permanent position of self-defence and in a position of never being understood. Your filtered view is causing you to fear the world, deny the world, and misinterpret the world. And the result is the painful and exhausting condition of constant reactivity.

So, how to look beyond the filter? There is only one way and that is to look from the eyes of the Heart; to become the witness to the filtered eyes. Heart-eyes have a clear view. They can see the whole view without personal preference. They are the witness to *all* the personal views, including the person you are calling you. To look from the eyes of the Heart is to look with panoramic vision; it is no longer to think as such. Instead, what emerges are arisings, knowings or thoughtless thoughts, the spontaneous and pure promptings of the Heart.

twelve

A PERSON who is looking through filtered eyes is defined by expectation. It can be no other way, for in believing oneself to be an island unto oneself, a person cannot help but feel in conscious and unconscious expectation of someone or something to complete them. Added to this broad human tendency, one person's expectations shall also contain within them their own unique flavour, dependent upon the person's filtered experiences. A person will then come up against other persons—each with their own personalised set of expectations. Initially, there may be some relief to have certain requirements met; but ultimately such meetings are unstable and will result in disappointment. Out of disappointment comes the learned understanding of love, a love that lets you down; a love that never answers up to its promise; a love that never fully completes. This in turn adds layers to the personality, layers that create each person's own reactive and self-protective universe.

There are many layers to you, many learned behaviours.

But there is no judgement of them. On the contrary, there is gratitude for each aspect of your personality. Each detail is part of the great jigsaw that serves to bring you into recognition of who you are. Each one's story is their script for returning Home. Nonetheless, to live a reactive and expectant existence is to be in constant suffering. To transcend this perception of the world takes a sharp eye, for you have to ask yourself: what expectations have been defining this personality? You have to be willing to stand as the witness to your story and investigate all those things that comprise a you.

To know yourself you have to be truthful in all things. This means active scrutiny of your behaviour; *not* other people's behaviour. If someone else's behaviour triggers something in you, upsets you, angers you, this is your perfect opportunity to ask: what is it in *me* that is triggered? What expectation in me has not been met? Only by bringing each aspect of yourself into the enquiry can you begin to understand it; only by reaching understanding can you release a tendency. So, begin by observing every trait as it arises. Observe without judgement, but with compassion for this one who is still in expectation. And there is only one way to observe without judgement, and with compassion, and that is to reside as You. To know Truth—to know You—is not separate from being truthful. Because you can only know what is truthful when you are residing as you Are, as Truth. Then, and only then, is the personality free to shine in all its beauty.

✑ thirteen ✑

TRUTH IS that which is ever so. Truth does not waver or change; it does not stop and temporarily become something else. What is true is true, permanently. It is what Is. It is the unchanging Reality.

To know Truth is to recognise the backdrop to all movement, to all change, to all that comes and goes. It is to know Existence that contains existence. To know Truth is to know the knowing that you know without knowing how you know. For how do you know that you exist? You cannot rationalise your sense of Existence. It is something that is known directly, that cannot be borne out of logic or analysis. The thinking mind knows only logic and analysis; it knows *ideas*. Ideas are subject to debate, they are mutable and unstable. The thinking mind knows only the changeability of experience. And within that changeable, thinking mind comes a strong preference for experiences that make the mind feel good. But the one who feels jubilant, the one who feels joyful, the one who has seen a beautiful sunset and is inspired by its beauty is equal in substance to the one who is fearful. None of these feelings are the essential You, the essential Truth. Even the one who feels overwhelmed with love for the world is not the essential You. This feeling, like all feelings, will come and then go. That is not to say you cannot enjoy these sensations when they come. Why not, enjoy! Only do not hold on to any feeling; this is when suffering begins.

You have no choice but to experience because you inhabit a body/mind. However, the minute the mind becomes *attached* to experience and defines itself by experience is the minute the mind becomes consumed by and identified with its own story. When we try to hold on to certain experiences, we find ourselves in a permanent position of disappointment and loss. We feel as if we are living on ever-shifting plates, a feeling which produces a great anxiety. We mourn the changeability of relative existence, and feel ourselves at its mercy. But the human being has a unique capacity. It can taste the Reality that never changes. All that is required is a switch of your attention. Turn your focus to that sense of Existence in you; that innate sense of Awareness-Being. Does Awareness ever leave, ever change? Is it not the case that every time you look, it is 'there'? Only the mind has the ability to wander, and it does so because it fears the Truth. Because to know the Truth is to know that you are no-thing. But fear is not the enemy; no feeling is the enemy. All is Consciousness arising to remind you of You. Reside as You are; only as You are. From the perspective of You, the wide spectrum of experience may be experienced in all its temporary beauty, while You remain, unchanging, as the Truth of I.

✍ fourteen ✍

WHY WOULD you not trust the One who loves you? Because it is easy for a child's mind to get distracted. It wants to experience so many things, meet so many new people, travel to faraway places. And why not? This is part of the mind's journey. But it is a folly to stay trapped in childhood. Young children are egocentric. They cannot imagine anything other than their mind's perspective.

You are being asked now to step into the *Watcher* of this mind, into your adulthood. The nature of this Watcher is to stand aside and observe its own child. It can see the tantrums and the determination the child has to get what it wants; it can see the disappointment and the feeling of abandonment when the child does not receive the attention it wants; it observes how wrapped up and unconscious the child really is. But the Watcher makes no judgement. It is not angry at its own child. It sees rather the perfection of the child's journey; that each tantrum somehow washes it further out of itself. It sees that each aspect of the child's story has somehow led it to this very moment of adulthood. It sees that nothing is wasted, nothing is lost, there is no hardship, there is no bad luck, there is no suffering. It sees that suffering is only a misunderstanding of Itself, and that misunderstanding has led the little one no longer to trust the One who loves them.

A perception of suffering and a lack of trust go hand in hand. Who is the one who feels they are suffering? Who is the one who feels a lack of trust? This is the one who can experience many feelings, moods and emotional states. This is the person who is committed to the personal experience. This commitment alone produces the states of suffering and a lack of trust. The person who has forgotten the One who holds them relies on new experiences to hold them. But all that comes will eventually go. So, for the one who is reliant on experiences to hold them, each departure will bring fresh suffering, fresh feelings of disappointment and abandonment. And so each new 'departure' adds a new layer of distrust, a deeper perception of suffering.

Now is the time to undo those layers. What is aware of your state of mind? Tune in to your own Awareness. Is the space of Awareness feeling anything? Is it troubled in any way? From the perspective of space there is no judgement of any 'state'. From this deeper view it is seen that suffering is only a misunderstanding of the Self, and that it comes so as to awaken each child.

~ fifteen ~

YOUR TASK is to tune in to the subtle current of your being. This is the gift of being human: the ability to tune in to the Great Resonance. This is the One Vibrational Tone out of which all of manifestation is born. To know peace is to know the Great Resonance that you are. Right now you can listen to the sound of Being. Put your hand over the centre of your chest and tune in to your own resonance. Begin with the space between hand and chest. Feel the vibration of this space; listen to the silence of this space. See if you can feel and hear the subtle *hum* of this space. To tune in to this hum is to tune in to the vibration of Consciousness-Existence itself. In every moment of every day you can hear the hum beyond all things. If you feel lost, tune in to the *hum of Existence*. If you feel empty, tune in to the hum of Existence; if you feel sad or stressed, tune in to the hum of Existence. If you are confused and don't know which way to turn, sit within and tune in to the hum of Existence. If you are angry or agitated, sit within and tune in to the hum of Existence.

If you are feeling happy, sit within and tune in to the hum of Existence.

Is the vibration of Existence *feeling* anything? Is it lost, does it feel empty, sad, stressed, confused; does it not know which way to turn? Is it angry or agitated; does it *feel* happy? Is this vibration of Existence coloured in any way, differentiated in any way? Now look to the quality of your feelings, feel *their* vibration. Each one shall have its own frequency. All feeling-frequencies will come and go. They appear and they disappear. And what a variety they contain! The entire palette of this Creation will appear in your awareness at one time or another; changeable vibrations vibrating within the One Vibration. But does the vibration of Existence come and go? Sit within and discover if what *Is* ever changes.

Who is the one who is forever changing? This one is your mind. The mind has become consumed by its own changeability. But now the time has come to know the one who is *aware* of all that diversity. Tune in to your sense of Existence; tune in to the Vibration of You. From this deeper perspective pure understanding emerges. The tighter your focus on the hum of Existence the more you will discover that you cannot separate yourself from the hum. You are one with the hum, for Existence is You.

~ sixteen ~

FEAR IS the very fabric of the identified mind. Fear itself is reliance on thoughts; reliance on the person to maintain you. The mind has spent a long time cultivating its idea of itself. It has spent a long time maintaining this kingdom called a mind. No matter the outward appearance of strength, to be in charge of a kingdom is to be in a position of permanent weakness. A kingdom has borders, and those whose reality is limited to their kingdom must seek to protect those borders from attack. And thus walls are built in defence and defiance. There are sentries at every gate-post of this mind-kingdom, determined to keep control and maintain autonomy. Maintaining control is the mind's only known way of survival; to relinquish control is synonymous with defeat, with weakness, with chaos, with *not understanding*. The mind seeks to know in concrete terms; it seeks to understand. What it cannot understand it doubts and avoids and fears.

And so it is that the more you come to the heart-space—the more you bathe in the Silence of your Being—the more fear will intensify. This is unavoidable. For how do you know this Silence? How is it that you know Love? This is the knowing that you know without knowing how you know. This is the wisdom that has gone beyond all rationality. It is therefore only natural the mind should put up a fight, for it is being asked to go beyond its very own logic; it is being asked to trust a knowing. Suddenly, everything that it has held on to and felt to understand comes apart at the seams. Nothing makes sense any more; what once felt certain is now on shaky ground. If, says the mind, I am stripped of all my thoughts, my memories, my hopes and desires, if I am stripped of my *kingdom*, then what is left? Such a question is to throw the fearful mind into an even deeper fear. But all is okay. All is just as it should be. For fear comes to push us over the edge, beyond those borders, into the heart of pure knowing.

∞ seventeen ∞

C AN YOU trust that there is no such thing as something 'bad'? There is only misunderstanding. Life throws us whatever lessons we need. Whatever arises is an opportunity for self-reflection. The mind does not always want to hear this. It assumes that remedies for the outside world must be sought. No such remedies will ever work in any profound way. Whatever emotions have arisen in response to these lessons, know that they are Life's gift to you, to help you come into a deeper understanding of yourself.

It may feel as if you are being admonished. But I am merely steering you; merely guiding. A mother does not want her child to hurt itself, so she lays boundaries. This you already know if you look within. Those boundaries healthy for your existence, healthy for your journey, are already set within your heart as your own loving reins. We have to pull the mind in, for it is a wilful, indeed obstreperous, child. And yet how better to communicate with a child than with love. If you shout, hurt or frighten a child, it will not understand.

Life is never shouting at you, no matter the strength of its voice. Can you see, it merely wishes to drown you in Love? Sometimes that drowning may be perceived as painful, but only if you struggle, only if you fight for breath.

No child likes to be called a baby. Every child actively grows away from babyhood, asserting its independence from Mother. This is natural and all part of a grand evolution. But part of that evolution involves a powerful denial of Mother's wisdom; a period in which the child dissociates and forgets its origin. Having forgotten Mother and the womb out of which it was born, the child now feels isolated. Even more crucially, the child now feels abandoned by Mother. A great anger arises at Life, an anger that Life is a cruel and unloving parent. And from this position, all that is misunderstood is perceived as 'bad'. There is only one way to remedy this sense of abandonment and that is to revert to infancy. How does it feel right now to be as an infant? Can you feel that inward sensation of babyhood? This baby cannot even lift its own head without Mother. It cannot walk or talk or make its own decisions. This baby is beyond even trust. It knows simply it is eternally held, eternally supported, eternally loved. Be willing to let yourself sink into the Mother's arms, and know that nothing occurs without your benefit at heart.

eighteen

DOER-SHIP CAUSES much confusion. Questions are asked, such as: well, how shall I do my work, get up out of bed, do the things that need to be done? The mind feels it must be pro-active and so it rushes ahead in order to seek, achieve and reach goals. It fears that without a goal in life it will be lost and without definition. But the truth is, the more we try to find 'personal definition', the more we find ourselves forever balancing the precarious seesaw of achievement versus failure, and the more lost to ourselves we become. The mind is rushing to define itself even without being conscious it is rushing. Its position is to be in a permanent state of self-declaration, a state of claiming its own existence: this is who I am, this is what I do, and this is how I do it. The mind fears that if it does not 'do' it will no longer be: I do not know who I am, it says, if I am without activity.

You will not be idle once you know who you are. The awakened mind sees intuitively what is to be done. You cannot avoid 'doing', because you have materialised into the phenomenon of cause and effect. Nonetheless, once you see that you are not the Doer, doing emerges without the movement of the goal-oriented mind. The work may be strenuous, it may require intense concentration; it may even have a quickened pace to it, but still there is no rusher. The work is done for its own sake, for love, in love, through love, as love.

In this moment, you can use your body to see who is 'doing'. Put your hand on the centre of your chest and feel the space between palm and chest. Allow yourself to sink into the space of Being. Now let space read these words. Let space hold the book. Let space type on the keyboard. Let space stand and walk across the room. What is the quality of your movement? Who is the one who is doing? Give your body to this formless space and see how activity flows from Silence itself. If there is ever to be one goal, it is to let space move you, talk you, breathe you, be you. This we can call Love in action.

❧ nineteen ❧

INERTIA AND doer-ship are two sides of the same coin. One gives the impetus for the other. Doer-ship eventually exhausts itself and collapses into inertia, while inertia feels it can only jump out of itself via the pushing energy of doer-ship. How is it we get stuck in such extremes? Inertia and doer-ship arise out of a misunderstanding with yourself, out of a misapprehension that you are the one in control of your existence. They arise only because you have forgotten your Self.

The person who feels they are primarily a person will always feel they are in charge of their life. The mind teaches that we must achieve, and that to achieve we must work hard towards a goal. There is both wisdom and misunderstanding in this teaching. Wisdom knows that the conscientious heart shall always work diligently. It has integrity for the task and performs all tasks for one sake only: for the sake of Love. Misunderstanding begins with the need for outcome. The heart is not dependent on outcome. It will be happy whatever the result. The mind, on the other hand, is entirely dependent on outcome. It has a goal to reach, a wish to uphold, and much energy will be exerted in trying to realise this goal. However, so often our wishes are not met. Life will move those goal-posts and not allow a dream to appear. The doing mind will keep on doing; trying to find new ways to attain its goal, until eventually it collapses into exhaustion, confusion and despondency. In that moment it is as if all the will has just been let out of the balloon, and there is no air left. This we can call inertia.

Inertia goes hand in hand with depression and anger. For a while there comes a feeling of not being bothered about anything. This then moves into defiance and determination to push for what was denied. The energy of this determination pushes through the stagnancy of inertia, and for a moment the mind feels exhilarated to be back on the wheel of doing. The mind feels fully in control once again, at the helm of its own ship, eager to set its own coordinates and have nothing get in its way.

What if the coordinates are not yours to set? What if this person who you believe yourself to be has no say, no will, no wheel of its own doing? In truth, it is *all* your will, but not the 'you' you have been committed to. Know the You that determines everything and you will see that pushing and collapsing occur only when you have forgotten this You. The heart does not push anything into existence. From the wisdom of the Heart, it is known when effort is required and effort is given effortlessly. So, the moment you feel the weight of inertia or the pushing of doer-ship, turn that spotlight inward. Tune in to the Silence of your Being and ask yourself: is Beingness *doing* anything, wanting anything, needing any outcome?

twenty

THE THINKING mind loves to taste new experiences and, as a result, jumps about, in between, never really settling. In the beginning it is necessary, for much learning is gained from all that experiencing. Every new-born throughout Creation must begin its journey into maturity by saturating itself with all the textures of its surroundings. Even in the most literal way, tasting is the first means of discovery. An infant's impulse is to put everything in its mouth! It is part of its learning to discriminate between things. What a perfect analogy that it should learn to decipher its surroundings by the sensitivity of its taste-buds. Every infant in every species must navigate its way through a dizzying array of sights and sounds, because it is through acute listening, seeing, touching and sensing that an infant begins its journey into the wisdom of discrimination. For now, it is firmly material and rooted in form; it has to be. Form must use its form to deepen its understanding of itself. And so, for now, this self feels entirely personal.

The result of so much tasting is not only a hunger for more stimuli, but also a gathering of preferred tastes. By the time the child has grown into adulthood, its idea of itself has become intimately related to the things it likes and the things it does not like. The adult now defines themselves by his or her preferences, so much so, that his or her idea of happiness is entirely dependent on finding things that are enjoyed and avoiding things that are not enjoyed. From here, a dissatisfaction grows. Even a good taste does not fully satisfy, and so the mind keeps on looking for satisfaction. Like a monkey, it jumps from tree to tree, searching for what it thinks to be the real fruit, yet never fully content with what it finds. Many years will pass in this way; and yet as frustrating as they may feel, they are not spent in vain. Far from it, for what teachings each piece of fruit yields. Each leap to each new taste is in fact leading you, through winding and extraordinary pathways, to that which is prior to all detail; leading you to know *Real Taste*, to know the You who is eternally watching the one who experiences.

To have a *Real Taste* of You is synonymous with what we can call coming to the Heart; it is to know this *prior-ness* that is you. It is to taste and to be the fundamental I that is beyond the sights and the sounds, beyond distinction; it is to taste the Love that is beyond all preference. The mind will keep jumping in fear of this I, for the light of this I is vast beyond all understanding. And yet all of that searching is ultimately to know this I beyond all. Look now and see if the Silence of your Being is searching for anything or wanting anything. What a taste is this Silence of You, so sublimely sweet, and free of all wants. For once you have tasted your Self, there shall be no other fruit that can compare to You.

twenty-one

NOTHING CAN make you feel anything. The trigger for feeling resides within you. No situation has the capacity to challenge you. If you are angered, hurt, upset or troubled, look within. You will discover that every 'challenging' situation you face is in fact a mirror to an aspect within you. It has come to help you release the one who can *be* challenged; to show you that whatever is going on outside is never the source of the challenge. To peel back the layers of this you, you must be willing to put yourself under the full glare of enquiry. What is it in me that feels angered, hurt, upset or troubled? Why do I feel this way? What misunderstanding lies within me?

The only thing that causes us to suffer is misunderstanding. Suffering arises from a misunderstanding with ourselves. Because we believe ourselves to be separate beings, we are constantly in a state of fear and a state of lack. We seek our own protection, consciously and unconsciously, because we are permanently seeing other beings as different and separate from us. They are the 'other' from whom we must protect ourselves. At the same time, and in seeming opposition to that, we look to the 'other' to complete us. This need for completion drives all of our actions, but of course such need can never be met. And when it is not met the mind feels hurt, angered, troubled and challenged. From these most fundamental misunderstandings about who you are arise all the challenges that you will ever face.

Don't worry about changing someone else's behaviour. It is time to stop pointing outwards and looking for answers outside of ourselves. Instead, we must turn that spotlight inward, with constant and compassionate vigilance for this one who is in misunderstanding. Who is it who is challenged, hurt, angered; who is it who is feeling this fear; who is it who is feeling this sense of lack? And is this one essentially me?

twenty-two

THE ONE who is holding on to an opinion is keeping you trapped. We hold our opinions close, for we feel they define us and make us distinct from another person. An assertion of opinion is an assertion of our existence: this is who I am, this is how I delineate myself from all other beings; my opinions confirm to me the kind of person I think I am. But, just for one moment can you be without opinion? What occurs? Are you less of what you were? Perhaps in the dropping of opinion you will discover more of you than any opinion could ever find.

That is not to say that you as a unique appearance shall not shine in your individuality. But do not try to run before you can walk. First, in order to shine as the individual, the individual must be surrendered, wholly. Be as an infant in its mother's arms, untutored, unconditioned. Be, for one moment, as helpless as that child and trust that the mother has everything it needs for its existence; everything it needs for happiness. You suffer because you have lost your faith in Mother; you do not trust that She will catch you.

You will not be lazy or undisciplined when you are as an infant in the Mother's arms, quite the opposite. Discipline will emerge naturally, to the point where it is no longer 'discipline'. But it is true, in the beginning the mind needs firm handling. The mind wants to stick to its opinions it has of itself, and reinforce itself via its opinions. So stand aside and observe an opinion as it arises. Feel its vibration. There is a tightened quality to a strong opinion; you can feel this tightening like a contraction within. Your opinion may feel certain of itself, but does it feel sincere? What happens when you allow that your opinion may be wrong? What happens when you tune in to the One Vibration and watch the opinion-vibration from there? Is the opinion as rooted, as sincere as you thought? Feel the space that comes when the tightening loosens, when your focus is on the Watcher of your opinion. That which is watching all opinion, You are.

twenty-three

WHO IS this one giving you guidance? It is none other than your own Self. You are learning to cultivate a relationship with your Self. This is the only relationship to cultivate, the one with the Divine. Discover who you are really wedded to, who you are really child to! This is the relationship you are aching for—the one with your own beloved Self. In every human being there is that spark of knowing, that inner voice. This is Heart's voice, the language of your deepest wisdom. This voice has never stopped talking to you; simply you have forgotten to listen. In the beginning, many beings hear this voice in another being. A day comes when suddenly that language is re-ignited in the heart, and they recognise the Divine Voice in a teacher, a master, an idol, a light. To hear this Voice is to fall into instant remembrance of the purest harmony. There is no doubt of the truth of that Voice, for it speaks in a way that is more familiar than your own skin.

To know this Voice as the Heart's voice is what we might call 'receiving guidance'. In the beginning, all beings must remain in 'receivership', because no mind wants to be subject to anyone or anything, least of all a higher wisdom. When the Heart's voice chimes inside, an extraordinary 'toppling' occurs. This is when we place all of our faith in our intuitive knowing, in our heart, and ignore the thinking mind that doubts. In the hearing and knowing of the One giving you guidance, you have bypassed the thinking logic of your mind. This is the first step on the road to Surrender. To really listen to this inner Voice, to have full faith in its truth, to give yourself entirely to this deeper wisdom is what we can call 'coming to the Heart'.

You cannot know your Self until you are subject to your Self. This means handing over this kingdom of your mind, and placing yourself at the feet of the Divine. This is only possible when that Voice has resonated so deeply in your being that there feels to be no other way than to listen.

twenty-four

WHAT IS yours? Can you pinpoint anything that belongs to you and be certain that it is yours? Who are you who feels entitled to own something? The root of ownership is the root of identification. You think you own this you who is residing in this body and this mind. But who are you to take ownership? You say, my body, my mind, but who are you who 'owns' this body, this mind?

What if, for one moment, I allow that this body, this mind does not *belong* to me? What occurs? Somehow it is as if the world has been disembowelled. Everything drops; a great emptying, and what remains is un-nameable. What remains cannot *own*, for it is not a some*thing* to possess another thing. What remains is without definition. No limit can be put on what remains. It has no boundary, no fixed point.

This is Home. This is the Real Estate that cannot be owned; the un-nameable, unbound I.

twenty-five

RIGHT NOW in this moment there is only one focus. Before you work out what to do, where to go and when to do it, focus here on *Now*. This is not a question of time. To live Now is not about living in a moment of time. Now-ness is beyond time, it is recognition of your divine Being. To be in the Now is to reside as pure Presence. The present moment occurs within Presence, within Now. In the Now the thinker of thoughts is relieved of all responsibility; there is no thinker of thoughts in the Now! You will no longer have to work out what to do, where to go and when to do it. Simply your feet will move, an inner momentum shall guide you forward, and whatever doing is required shall intuitively be seen.

Many beings focus their meditation on bringing their attention fully into the present moment. This is a vital first step. We must begin with *concentration*. Let us say you are washing the dishes. Historically, you have done the dishes whilst thinking of a million other things to do. The washing has been rushed and wished away. You have run ahead of this present moment in favour of a better moment. So to bring the attention fully to the washing of each dish is to settle the mind and pull its focus inward. However, as essential as this moment of concentration is, it is still locked in a moment of time. The next step is to take yourself into *contemplation*.

Many sensations shall be felt in the act of washing the dishes, all occurring simultaneously. But now you can ask: who is *aware* of all this sensation? Now you can tune in to Awareness itself. Can you touch your Awareness? Is it visible, is it male or female, does it have a limit, is Awareness washing the dishes? You can see and feel the activity in your hands, but is the Awareness of that activity active? What occurs to your movement when your focus is taken beyond the present action and into the witness of it? Such questions we can call contemplation. Now you are moving from present to Presence; from you to You, from here to Now. Such contemplation takes you beyond. It takes you into what we can call real *meditation*: the bathing in the timelessness of You. From this deeper seeing there is only Awareness, only Now, only the Doer who is doing nothing.

twenty-six

HOW IS IT that you can feel such expansiveness of Being; how is it that you can feel a Love beyond anything you have ever known, and still feel lost in a maelstrom? Why does the one who is protesting and berating and charging up and down the corridors of your mind seem to be getting louder and louder? It can seem to make no sense that such intensity of Love can be felt, only then to drop into such intensity of despair. The truth is, the more you come to the Heart, the more the mind will initially rage. There is nothing more painful to the mind than to know Real Love, because Love makes you face every aspect of your personal self. And this hurts the mind, and makes it want to run and hide. But all is well. Your task is to take your mind by the hand, and gently, but firmly, steer it into your Conscience.

The Conscience is your inner Voice—the Heart-Voice. It is your innate wisdom. The forgetting of the Self is the forgetting of the Conscience. All beings must forget for a time, until the moment comes to remember. But to remember your

Self fully, you must be willing to feel pain; you must be willing to go into the storm of your emotions and face each one. Even a storm—even in the height of its misunderstanding—has come to help you remember. Often, it takes the full power of a storm to awaken us. The secret is to watch the tempest without becoming one with it. In the beginning, that may mean a simple stepping aside so that you do not overspill onto others. Allow the protest without giving it to others. Remember that every action leaves an energetic footprint. So, sit by yourself, go for a run, beat the pillow, scream in a field. In that way, whatever needs to come to the surface may be exposed safely and given its due space. But you will not sink so as to be lost in the maelstrom.

From this distance you can look to the details without getting lost in the details. See if you can identify the source of the protest. Something must require your attention for it to protest so loudly. This is why you need never fear a storm. Those dark clouds are not the enemy. They fill to bursting for very good reason: to water and purify your being. How a storm will clear the airways, blow through all manner of stagnation and allow you to see with clear vision. Even as the mind is rampaging, you are being taught to remain as the silent observer, lovingly compassionate, sincerely detached. The mind is *not* your enemy; only your attachment to and identification with your mind causes pain. So, use your protesting as a means of purifying this mind. Thus, with rigorous and painstaking study you may bring every aspect of this personality under your microscope of love.

twenty-seven

DO NOT deny feelings when they come. Allow them to speak to you. Only do not get caught in their web. This can be tricky. For in their arrival, feelings must be felt. Your task is to feel without becoming tainted and overwhelmed. Feelings must be brought under Your loving microscope and dissected. No one can make you feel anything. If you feel hurt or upset by someone else's behaviour then this is your opportunity to find out who is this one who has been hurt, who is this one who is upset? What is it in myself that has allowed this feeling? It is like taking your psyche on the deepest of archaeological digs. Each artefact, no matter how arcane, must eventually be brought under the knife of your awareness. In this way, you may see all the aspects of the personality in fine detail. Only by understanding them may you release them back to Source with loving gratitude for their appearance. Only by understanding them may your personality shine, effulgent. This is how we may *purify* the mind, for without this dissection your own details are blocking your view.

So, how is it that your view can be blocked? Now that you are realising the formlessness of Being, you may begin to see the reality of the body/mind mechanism. Can you tune in right now to your sense of Being? Tune in to the formlessness of You, to the You that cannot be circumscribed. To sink here is to go beyond all thought, to go beyond your body. The thinking mind is continually investing in a new attraction. Investment arises from ingrained thought-patterns, and it is these which are blocking your view of your Self. They are all the layers of reactivity within you; which is to say, all the ideas you have about your *personal* self. Your personal view is formed out of your experiences, which in themselves are carved out of your personal needs, wants and projections. This view can never be Impersonal, for it is too wholly imbedded in the personal needs. Each being has their own script of thought-patterns, tendencies and traits—their own script of need; an entire world constructed out of need. When you are focused only on the script you cannot know the Great Writer of that script. To know the Writer is to see the exquisite precision of His pen, for through each trait, each lovingly written tendency, you are being shown the You beyond all tendency.

Love has given you the capacity to feel feelings as a stepping stone to feeling the Love-Self; to know your Self as the Writer of all. So do not deny feelings when they come. Simply dig, so that all may be seen in the clarity of You. Know that you are held in this process; each step is a Divine step. Your first task is to hand yourself over. Put your feelings in Heart's palm. What a softening of possibility! Only now from the Heart may this auspicious enquiry begin.

56

twenty-eight

WE HAVE said that Truth is that which is ever so; that Truth is the unchanging reality. We know that feelings come and go, that they are forever inconstant. From this perspective it would seem they are not the *fundamental* Truth. The question may come: if feelings are not real then perhaps they do not matter; and if they do not matter, then why should I investigate them? What matters is this: are you comfortable with yourself? When you stand before the mirror, what do you see? Can you be certain that all actions today flowed from love? Are there some areas that feel murky, less clear, more agitated, uncomfortable? If so, go there. Investigate what is causing this agitation. What textures are forming this you? Are not some so subtle that you do not even have names for them? There is nothing to fear in looking. Fear is one of those textures; it is an aspect appearing in You.

Is an aspect of you separate from You? Remember that all movement-vibrations occur within the One Vibration. Therefore, can we ever say that movements are not real?

Movements are Truth in the form of movements. In the same way that ripples in water are still formed out of water, so too aspects of Consciousness are made of the same substance. They appear and they disappear within their own reality. Therefore, to deny the reality of feelings is to create further ripples of misunderstanding. This is why awakening to the Self is just the first step. From a deeper wisdom you can now begin to see all the ways in which you have limited your view.

In an absolute sense there is nothing to clear, nothing to remove. What you are is eternally pure, without obstruction. But your vision of your Self has become coloured with ideas. So, what is being asked by standing in front of the mirror and investigating the personality and all its textures? Merely that in coming home to your true nature the mind will continue to hold on tenaciously to everything it thinks it knows. It will delude you into thinking it is clear. Your task in front of the mirror is to stand as a stern but loving teacher before a class of unruly pupils. Your silence alone is enough to make them sit still! Each pupil will be forced to go within and investigate their unruly behaviour in the light and compassion of the Teacher. All your textures will thus be combed through via the gentle precision of the Teacher.

twenty-nine

THE MIND is quick to judge itself. I am so weak, it says. It is full of self-hatred for what it perceives as weakness. Weakness may be defined as that which has momentarily become insincere. Self-hatred arises when we turn our backs on our own goodness. Human beings deny their own goodness and spend lifetimes pursuing their desires. Desires melt when you remember your own goodness, which is why for as long as desires are leading the way, the human being must forget its own goodness. This is the cycle of the thinking mind— to be full of desire so as to find completion, to ignore the goodness of the Conscience in the pursuit of the desire, and accordingly to be filled with unconscious self-loathing for denying goodness, and for being 'weak'.

How do you know goodness? Eat this question, and see if it can be answered. You know what is good and pure without knowing how you know. This is real wisdom; this is Real Knowledge. To listen to the deepest wisdom of your Conscience is to know the Goodness that you are. When you are residing as the Goodness that you are, nothing can escape your attention. When the mind is being insincere you can feel it inside. It hurts to be insincere. You are therefore your very own barometer. This barometer is never in judgement; it is never condemning your insincerity, but it is firm in its clarity. The barometer of Love shall take each of your weaknesses under its wing of compassion and firmly unpeel them. Can you see that what you once felt as weakness has now become your great strength? For it is by investigating all that comprises and encourages your insincerity that you will come into a greater understanding of yourself.

Sincerity speaks only one language, that of purity. The path of purity is the path of sincerity; the path of love is the path of sincerity; the path of understanding is the path of sincerity. You are sincerity itself. Let go of everything but the sense of Existence. Put your focus here. Only then may you discover the sincerity that you are. For Existence itself is Sincerity.

✑ thirty ✑

THE MORE I bathe in the Silence of my Being, the more I discover I cannot circumscribe my Self. I see no limit to the Silence of I. But if I have no limit, then surely there is only I. If I have no limit then I am eternally one with myself. And what is one with itself cannot see itself. Just as my physical eye cannot see itself without a mirror, so I cannot see I without a mirror. This is the nature of the mind-I: a mirror to the Eternal-I.

Now I am realising the magnificence of this little mind-I. The little-I is a mirror to Awareness-I. For I see that I am able to experience my limitless Self only *through this mind*. This is why the mind matters, why the mirror that is the mind must be clear. Without a clear mind-mirror, my view of my Self is blocked. This is why I must look to my mirror to see all the ways in which I have limited my view. These ways are everything I am holding on to: my thoughts, my ideas, my memories, my experiences, my hopes, my desires, everything that has so far comprised this personal-I. These are the clouds on my mirror-sky. Only when the clouds have dissolved in the sun can you see the sky that contains them.

Do not delay in shining consciously. You are here to become aware of your Awareness, which is to shine a pure image back to You. In this way, I may witness My own effulgence.

thirty-one

S O FAR 'heart' and 'mind' have been separated so that it may be seen you are not primarily your thoughts. But the mind is far from being the enemy; the reality is that everything is Mind. The *thinking mind* is the aspect within the Great *Mind* of Consciousness that has temporarily forgotten its Greatness. Mind of itself is inherently pure. Simply, the One Mind has split itself into countless versions of Itself. Each version, or individual mind-self, is the means through which Great Mind-Self may witness Itself. But this 'splitting' contains much complexity, for within the capacity to become self-aware, Consciousness has also created the capacity to forget itself temporarily; to *not* seemingly be self-aware. This might seem curious; why, it could be asked, would Consciousness have created a capacity to deny Itself?

Imagine Consciousness as a diamond. Each of its facets is one of its creations; all the you's and me's within existence. When you are in the presence of a being who is whole-hearted, you feel their presence; you feel Love emanating from them;

you feel their heightened vibration. The 'whole-hearted facet' is the one who is shining with clarity. Imagine the brilliance of the Diamond when all of its facets are shining at their fullest. To experience a whole-hearted being is to know at once the potential of this Diamond—a potential, vast beyond all imagining. And so it is that Consciousness itself is evolving; evolving—just like every parent—through its own children.

The thinking mind, therefore, has a very important role to play. It must forget, for what a remembering it is! It must become consumed momentarily by its own unique detail. It must forge forward in what feels to be possession of its own autonomy; like every child, it must attempt to strike out on its own, so as finally to reach a deeper synthesis with its own parental wisdom. Every evolution equals a journey; and this journey cannot be rushed. A critical point must be reached, usually when the forging forward exhausts itself. Only then, when the individual mind-self learns to focus its attention on the Watcher of its own thought-processes, is it able to gain distance from its thinking, and therefore from itself. To tune in to this distance—to this space of the Watcher—is to *be* the Watcher of all movement. Be the Watcher and you shall shine as the Clarity that you are.

thirty-two

HUMAN BEINGS are carrying a great weight of grief. When a human being begins to awaken to the Heart, they often experience intense grief. Many will say that their heart feels overwhelmed with sadness. Tears come; it can feel as if they will never stop. It may not even be clear why such tears are coming, but they fall nonetheless; tears that tear the whole world apart.

It can feel very confusing to feel such intensity of sadness and not to know what you are sad about. It is especially confusing to have tasted such purity of Love and then to feel burdened by this unknown grief. This is the grief of amnesia; the grief of separation; the grief of a child at having lost its parent; the grief of forgetting the Self.

There are added layers to this grief within the human psyche; layers of self-hatred at having turned away from the Parent; layers of unworthiness; layers of feeling undeserving of love; layers of anger towards the Parent for having abandoned its child. Each of these aspects will be faced in time, but for now it is enough to grieve; it is enough to cry. Those tears must come. Allow them to empty you out onto the floor. Allow grief to express itself through your form so that the dam in bursting may fully empty itself.

This grief is a part of waking up. It is a part of facing your own Reality. For in knowing what you are grieving for, it is seen with unwavering clarity that you shall never be able to turn your back on your Self again. This is Love's way of reaching you, to alert you to that which can no longer be denied.

thirty-three

TO BELIEVE is to go ahead of your Self; to imagine is to go ahead of your Self; to *think* is to go ahead of your Self. Belief in thought keeps you isolated and delineated: this is 'me' and this is 'you'. It confirms that you are a person in control of yourself; that you are a person separate and distinct from other persons. To know happiness is to go beyond belief, which means relinquishing this person you feel you know so well. In letting go of the 'me' you shall discover 'I'.

The mind will put up a fight. It has held on for so long and has enjoyed its own creation. This creation is not wrong; it is the natural and beautiful consequence of being human. But ultimately, every child must grow up and away from the Parent to *become* Parent. And in the developing years, this child does not want to be reminded of the Parent; it actively avoids Its authority and asserts its own individuality. These years are rich years, full of lessons learned. But, nonetheless, this assertion will one day exhaust itself. The effort to maintain control of the person and all that surrounds it collapses. And so the person has no choice but to let it all drop. He hands himself over, willing to say, I am wrong. My person is wrong about everything. My person has kept me tied to just an *idea* of who I am. And what a collapse this is! For to renounce ideas and the lover of ideas is to be as helpless and as unconditioned as an infant.

Does an infant know what is best for itself? Does an infant worry or try to figure out? Does an infant understand anything or try to understand? Does it plan; does it ask why; does it predict; does it set up contingencies; does it think that it has made mistakes, and fill itself with regret? Does it hope for the future or imagine other scenarios; does it desire and want and wish and dream? An infant has not yet learned to differentiate, and so cannot yet imagine anything other than its own self. Be as that infant. Be as helpless as that infant. An infant does not look for its own welfare. It does not ask how or when the mother will provide. It does not even trust. It is beyond trust. Be as a child in the lap of the Mother and see if, in any way, you are not provided for. You will see that to be as that infant is to reside as your Self; as Innocence, as Purity, as the Love that you are. You will see that to be as a child in the arms of the Mother is, paradoxically, to *be* Mother.

thirty-four

WHAT IS an intuition? It is a knowing that you know without knowing how you know. It is what occurs when you have stepped away from the one who *thinks* they know; it is the wisdom that emerges from the silence of the Heart. Intuition arises when the mind is no longer immersed in its thoughts. Only when you listen to the Silence of your Being may you 'receive' the frequency we call intuition; the knowing that you know without knowing how you know.

Coming to the Heart is a tuning-in to your intuitive knowing. In the beginning, intuition appears like a chink of light in a thick stone wall. The wall of the psyche is dense and seemingly impenetrable, yet that chink has nonetheless made its way through. And its brightness is what causes a human being finally to listen, to listen to the wisdom of its own intuitive knowing. That chink of light will appear in countless ways to get your attention. There is no limit to the creativity of Consciousness, and each new chink shall be brighter than the last.

For certain, though, as soon as the listening begins, so the doubting mind asserts itself. It will say: but this is madness, this is unstable, this is irrational; *I don't believe it.* Every human being must face its own disbelief. What you are is beyond belief. Do you believe you exist, or do you know you exist? Do you believe in love, or do you *know* love? Do you believe in goodness, or do you *know* goodness? The mind will rise up and call your knowing madness; the mind in the shape of your form and many forms will denounce what is true. But this is the teaching. To stand in a room of disbelief and doubt and not wobble is of itself an act of Love. To know intuitively is to know without knowing how you know. Such knowing cannot be explained, justified or rationalised. So, of course, the mind will seek to undermine what it cannot explain. Your task is simply to listen. Let your attention be caught. Let that spark of light wrap itself tightly around your heart and be willing to say: I don't know how I know this Love, but I know it.

thirty-five

*L*ET YOUR eyes be dazzled by Love. When a being is first exposed to themselves, the sight is so startling that for some it is as if they had been stupefied. To be stupefied is to be, in a way, under a spell of enchantment. But this enchantment is the true definition of magic. What is 'magic' but the spontaneous appearance of form? The very nature of Reality is its capacity to materialise spontaneously. Therefore, in the truest sense, to be enchanted is to have recognised That out of which all is born. Love has to cast a very powerful spell in order to get Its own attention. And so it is that, in the beginning, beings are seen to be love-struck. A force stronger than the most powerful magnet draws them to sit in the presence of Love, and there is nothing to be done but be magnetised. Doubts may come that something is wrong, that the mind is being hijacked and hoodwinked. Hoodwinked, no; hijacked, yes. For most beings, it takes a hijacking to wake up to who we are. Hoodwinking is what happens when we deny the truth of the enchantment, and turn our backs on Real Love.

Within this period of bedazzlement, the human being enters heightened states of both euphoria and despair. To the outside world it looks precarious, even frightening, in its instability. It is true that the mind becomes unstable for a while; it is true that behaviour can look and feel heightened; it is true that it can look and feel as if a human being has been utterly collapsed to life and to themselves. They have been; that is the Grace of bedazzlement. This period of 'collapse' is the most beautiful and powerful thing that can ever happen to a human being. To be hijacked by Love is to be knocked off all bearings. Like a ship on high seas, tossed about on this wave and that, there is for a time no steadiness, no mooring, no equilibrium. There is no avoiding the sea-sickness, just as there is no avoiding those tumultuous waves. They shall break you in every conceivable way. This is the Divine Enchantment: breaking your heart so that you may come to know your Heart.

thirty-six

WHAT DOES it mean to be magnetised? To be magnetised is to fall at the feet of Love. It is to see Truth, and to know that there is only one place to be. It is to have no choice but to be where you are, as you are. The attraction to Love is unstoppable in its force. This is because Love witnesses Itself and in that recognition is now incapable of being separated. To know this Love is to find what you have been searching for throughout lifetimes.

To be magnetised is to be pinned to the floor of Love. The arms and legs will kick and punch. They will try their hardest to escape the magnetic hold. They will recoil from the intensity of Love and cry for release. But it is no good. When the magnet comes it is unassailable. It comes so as to pin you down. If Love did not express as a magnetic force, your mind would not listen, it would have no impetus to remember.

To be magnetised is to be like a moth that is drawn to the light. The moth cannot help itself. It flies so close as to scorch its wings; it blinds itself; it is giddy and drunk on the radiance of light. It knows that there is no choice but to allow itself to be burned to the core. The burn is as heady and intoxicating as it is painful and terrifying. But to be magnetised is also to sober up to yourself. Giddiness goes, inebriation passes and what is left is clear, still, awake.

thirty-seven

WHAT IS devotion? Devotion is the result of pure seeing. Devotion is the unavoidable result of a direct experience of Unconditional Love. It is the seeing of the Reality in another, and in that seeing the mind is collapsed. It is the seeing that surpasses all doubt. And so, to be devoted is to transcend the rational mind. For in the experience of Unconditional Love you come to the knowing that you know without knowing how you know. There can be no way of explaining this Love. Devotion can only be understood when it is your own direct experience. If someone were to ask but how can you be so sure of this love, the only response is: I don't know, but I know. There can be therefore no truer expression of the Reality than that of a devotee towards Unconditional Love.

A devotee does not know why he is devoted to his Master. He does not question it. In the Master he sees absolute purity; a love that has no demand, no expectation, no need. In the Master's love he feels as a child, eternally held, eternally understood, eternally guided. In the love of the Master, the devotee has gone beyond even trust. He has put himself in his Master's arms, like an infant. He knows the Master knows him better than he knows himself; he knows that he will never be able to get away with anything. The devotee knows he shall be destroyed. In the terror of that knowing, still he places himself at the Master's feet. He has, in fact, no choice. Devotion is not a choice; it is not a wilful act. It is a transcendence of will, a transcendence of all dependence on the thinking mind, an absolute prostration to a manifestation of Pure Love.

thirty-eight

THE HEART-SEEKING mind knows its salvation lies in surrender. But there is no single definitive action that you can take which equals surrender. Surrender is the inward experience of a shift of perspective. If you place your hand on the centre of your chest, if you bring your eyes to beneath your hand, what happens in you? To look from the eyes of the Heart is to go beyond the person who thinks they must surrender. The person is not wrong as such, but you cannot *think* yourself into surrender. That is a contradiction in terms. Surrender is the natural consequence of being heart-centred. It is the mind fallen into the Heart; and when your mind has dropped into the Heart, you are no longer thought-driven. If we were to associate any action with surrender it would be the active inward reminder to bring that wandering mind back into the silence of the Heart. The mind will jump from thought to emotion to feeling to sensation so that it never has to stop, so that it never has to come to silence. This is why we must lovingly, but firmly, take charge of our mind.

Diverting your attention from thoughts to your heart shall, of its own doing, bring you to Silence. This is why 'letting go'—or surrender—remains a concept until you drop your focus to the Heart. Then everything drops in the non-doing recognition of the Heart.

To be heart-centred is to hand over control of your existence. It is to have raised the white flag and no longer to be in charge of this army of thoughts. Surrender can only be unconditional; it can only be absolute prostration; it can only be a full and unequivocal laying down of your arms. After all that inner warring for freedom amongst your thoughts, now you may finally realise the Freedom beyond your thoughts.

thirty-nine

IN ALL ACTION there must be integrity. The word 'integrity' encompasses everything. If you are uncertain, ask yourself: what would Love do? In the end, you have to answer to your heart and know that you have acted purely, sincerely, rightly. The Heart knows precisely what is to be done. There is no need to figure out or wrestle with options; not when you are tuned in to your own frequency. This is the frequency of Being, of the Love that you are.

It is as if you were tuning in to a radio station. This radio station is the station of Love, the station of I. To know this frequency is to listen with a deeper ear. It takes listening with your entire being. It cannot even rightly be called 'listening', for that implies action. It is rather that you reside as you are, simply, in the Heart; in the Heart of intuitive knowing. All the answers to all your questions lie here. What bounty is to be unearthed when you stop looking and merely reside.

There is no requirement to *have* integrity when you know who you are; integrity is the flavour of your innate being.

Nonetheless, in the peeling of our layers we must practise vigilance, for the mind is ever eager to step ahead of itself and to lay out what it thinks it knows best. This is your opportunity to draw yourself inward and to ask: is this behaviour coming from Purity, from Love, from Integrity; is this behaviour flowing from I?

forty

PATHY ARISES when we silence our innate sense of integrity. It is understandable the mind should want to silence it, because integrity itself is wholly overwhelming to the mind. Integrity is never serving personal need; it serves what is true, and that means the mind is left unfulfilled. It takes the humility of a lion to witness the mind in its desire to have its needs met and *not* to meet them. The choice to meet them is costly. For in the seeing of what is right, and in the mind fighting what is right and then turning its back on what is right, a great swathe of apathy can fall. This is the apathy that is born of self-hatred; the deep disgust at oneself for not doing what is good and true. This then coincides with the apathy that arises from exhaustion. The more we give in to fulfilling the desires of the mind, the more we feed the mind's hunger to take control of life. The need for control demonstrates itself in the pursuit of goals, and more often than not these goals are thwarted. The mind then pursues another avenue, determined upon its mission until eventually, exhausted and depleted, feeling insignificant and without power in a vast and seemingly cold universe, the mind gives up and sinks into despair and apathy.

There will be many branches, but the main root of apathy stems from a sense of isolation. Belief in oneself as an isolated being, separate from other beings, leads to a sense of responsibility for one's life: a sense that you must maintain yourself because no one else is there to support you. But again, no matter how hard you try, it feels as if life is working against you in your efforts. And so you sink into hopelessness which in turn leads to apathy. So, how to prevent this cycle from perpetuating itself? Can you for a moment become like an infant and hand over complete responsibility for your life? Can you let go of the reins of your existence and allow that the Mother will provide for your every need?

An infant is beyond trust. It has no preconceptions, no assumptions, no expectations. In this pure state growth occurs. There is a fear in the adult mind that 'handing over' is a sign of laziness. But think of the remarkable creativity that is spurred in the non-goal-oriented infant. An infant absorbs so easily because it has no expectations. It gives effort, spontaneously and freely. There is no laziness in surrender. It is quite the opposite. The purified mind knows what is to be done. Effort occurs effortlessly, without expectation, without demand, without wishing anything in return for effort. Apathy is the result of believing yourself to be driving this existence. It is time to take your hands off the steering wheel, to become the passenger as opposed to the driver and to see if, in any way, you are unfulfilled.

ꙮ forty-one ꙮ

I T IS NOT about doing nothing, but letting Nothing do. Which is what we might call the Divine Impetus. This impetus can have incredible force. It *is* force, which is to say, it is the Creative Force itself, so there is no limit to its potential. When we are surrendered wholly to it, the Force is then free to express through the form—which is when True movement occurs.

The mind feels that its first responsibility is to take responsibility. But who do you think is moving this body, writing these words, thinking these thoughts even? For what you are personally cannot be separated from what you are Impersonally. It is only your mind that separates them and imagines them to be unconnected. Your personality is not the baddie in this drama. Merely, your attachment to the personality is playing the role of the baddie. In fact, this baddie is playing his role most assiduously for a very good reason. He plays it so that you will come to discover your true nature; so that you will come to discover that this attachment to your personality is spoiling the plotline, driving it into cul-de-sacs, suffocating the life blood, drowning your creative flow.

And why? Because as long as there is someone who believes they are orchestrating the action, it is as if the airways have been blocked. All that is required is a sincere handing-over of this doer. You are the passenger and I am the One who steers you, always. So what have you to worry about? What is there for you to control or determine? This is where the misunderstanding lies. It is not that doing does not happen; only that when you are in perfect recognition of who you are, what is to be done becomes obvious, clear, effortless. Doing is done effortlessly, for you are but the means through which the Divine Impetus plays. What freedom in this dance! How this personality-I shall dance, free and unperturbed by desire, in the deeper wisdom of I.

forty-two

TO SPEAK of receiving intuition means there must be something capable of receiving. The one who receives is also *mind*—simply the purified aspect. This is the one who is in recognition of a deeper I; who is no longer identified as a thinker of thoughts. Imagine Consciousness as a vast computer hard drive. Each appearance within Consciousness is like a piece of software within the hard drive. When a human being is identified as being a human being, they forget the existence of the hard drive and believe that their own specifically written piece of software is the only reality. To become conscious of Consciousness is to become aware of the hard drive as the *essential* reality. It is to realise that the software cannot exist by itself; that it cannot work without the motherboard. Once you know yourself to *be* the motherboard, your entire perspective changes. You are then in recognition of the vast Intelligence of I. This I not only contains all the information of all the software, it is the capacity to write all information, and it is the backdrop upon which all information can appear. To know the vast Intelligence of I is therefore to have access to all the data. The purified mind, in having finally transcended its personal perspective, can now view everything from the original perspective, and thus can pick up on data that would otherwise have been missed. This data is what we experience as intuition.

However, even after recognising the essential reality, the human mind is still not completely steady in itself. It takes time to unravel the personal layers; they will not disappear overnight. The thinking mind and its personal viewpoint will still be in existence. And at this point, while it is in the process of being melted, the thinking mind shall be quick to jump in upon a pure knowing with a wish to see it into form. The thinking mind's natural position is a need to feel in control and to determine outcomes. It will want to own and hold on to this new-found understanding. But this is the moment for vigilance. This is when we see that even the most subtle of intuitions must be renounced the moment it arrives. Otherwise we shall have moved out of the realm of intuitive knowing and into the realm of the mind-pusher. Both are aspects within Great Mind. The thinking mind is that aspect that has forgotten its innate reality, and the purified mind is the aspect that has remembered its innate reality. The more you remember, the more your mirror to your Self is cleared of all limitation, and the more you are free to shine a pure image of your Self. What a powerful means to strip you clean, to hand over even your intuitive knowing, to allow whatever is yours in this life to appear in its own time, and so root your mind in its inherent purity.

∝ forty-three ∝

EVEN AS you eat you are eating within the presence of I; even as you talk you are talking within the presence of I; even as you look you are looking within the presence of I. Even in the act of breathing you are breathing within the presence of I. I is neither here nor there, far nor close. I is all-encompassing. How can you stray from I when this physical-you emerges from I? It is only that your attention has strayed. If you wish to know who this I is, then you must become the Watcher of your attention. See how your attention darts from one thing to another, see how hungrily it seeks diversion, how quickly it becomes bored and longs for another experience. We seek experience in order to fill what feels like a void in our lives. There is no void, there is only forgetfulness. If you wish to remember who you are, watch this seeker of experience; watch the one who eats, talks, looks, breathes; watch the one who *thinks*. As the dispassionate observer the world will play before your eyes, while you remain untouched.

This you who remains untouched, is it a see-able you? Is

this you eating, talking, thinking, breathing? Or is it merely the observer of movement? Take hold of your attention, turn it inward and shine its light on this you. Can you find you? This simple shift of perspective shall undo the one you think yourself to be. This one you think yourself to be has exhausted you. The personality does not have to be exhausting; it is only exhausting when we believe ourselves to *be* the personality. Belief attracts more belief until you are weighed down and curtailed by belief. This 'weighing down' can feel like being trapped in a dark cave without light. But all is well; the personality must begin its journey by limiting itself to this confined space. For what a gift Life has in store. A tipping point will come when Love can no longer contain itself. It shall spill into that cave and shine its light into every corner. Let it overspill, no matter how overwhelming, for Love wants you to be free, to discover that you are that which is witnessing this personality. Then you may play, consciously within the presence of I.

forty-four

WHEN YOU are willing, Love will move mountains. Willingness is your magical agent; it is the transformative key that opens the doorway into your heart. That one 'yes' to Love shall reveal the magnificence of Love in all its forms. You will find Love talking to you in a million different ways. Your eyes will take on a whole new language. They shall see Love talking in the smallest detail. A passing cloud will have a conversation with you; a bumblebee will point you in the right direction; a song on the radio will whisper its holy message into your lungs, with direct and joyful precision. You shall be breathing an entirely new universe; and you shall know it to be the first pure breath you have ever taken.

When you are willing, there is space. When you are willing there is space to be wrong; there is space to unpick the threads of your existence and not to mind being unpicked. Willingness unbuttons you while allowing you to feel the warmth of its embrace. Willingness allows fear to come; it knows that fear is the greatest gift within this existence, for it sees how fear pummels you into Freedom. Willingness does not mind what Love brings, even when something feels challenging. Willingness knows that a challenge can only come to the one who can still be challenged, and that therefore everything that comes is a gift of purification.

To be willing is to say: whatever it takes, however long it takes. It is not to answer Love back, or to say that Love has got it wrong. It is to lay oneself before Love's blade and to say whatever may be blocking my view, please remove it so that I may be free. Willingly, humbly and without reservation, this is your offering, this is your prayer: please purify this one until nothing remains but the Love that I am.

forty-five

KEEP AN eye out for the talkative one. Talking takes you outwards. We use words as a distraction. Their noise obscures the One who speaks without words. Wait until Love knows what to say. Love speaks a beautiful language. These words do not arise from thinking. Thinking hurries and so misses Real language. Thinking words are always locked in time; their scope is limited, their focus is personal. Thinking words bring judgement; inward judgement and outward judgement. Thinking words arise from a dependence on thoughts; they arise from not residing as you are. Step away from your thinking mind and become the observer to the thoughts and to the words that dart back and forth. The more you observe the less you will think; the less you think the less you will be filled with thinking words.

Love speaks without knowing what it will say next. It ushers forth whatever is required in a given moment. It knows beyond knowing when to stay silent. It knows beyond knowing when to say no. Love may speak firmly; it may even appear as a knife in its acuity, for Truth will express Itself in order to free itself from untruth. But these words are not hard and unyielding; they do not cut to be cruel. Even spoken, these words come from Silence; they *are* Silence, they are Love, they are Purity. The mind may momentarily hurt, because no mind wants to be told that it is no-thing. It will do whatever it can to hold on to its idea of itself. If words hurt you go to that place that got hurt and undo that. From that perspective all words, even thinking words, come to bring you back to your Self. The more you dissect the words of this personality, the more you will speak the language of the Heart.

forty-six

CHATTER—inward and outward—only becomes chatter when we lose our bearings. It is possible to contribute and participate without losing our position. We constantly change ourselves to accommodate each new situation. We rush in to please or be liked. This is when the chatter begins. It is as if you were a tree trunk that has lost its roots. With every gust it wobbles and moves without ever knowing its innate position. As a result its entire structure is insecure. It may fall at any moment. To calm this inner wobble we must keep ourselves rooted within our own being. In this way, residing as you are, you are able to meet any person, any situation without straying for one moment from who you are. The one who knows who they are is who they are with everyone they meet. In this being the roots are firm, but the trunk of knowing keeps the tree of life pliant, loose, and free to grow. Thus, outer turbulence will never be met by inner turbulence.

Inner turbulence arises out of not being sure of ourselves. To be sure of ourselves does not mean to be sure of the personality. In fact, the more we think ourselves to be sure of ourselves personally, the less sure we are of our Self, and the more turbulence is experienced. So, how to be sure of our Self? Draw that chattering mind inward. Focus in on that innate sense of Existence within you. Ask yourself, *as what* am I? This question shall bring you to the roots of You. This question shall silence all chatter. This question shall bring the discovery that You as Existence are untouchable, unknowable, unquantifiable. You *are* Existence in the form of you, of me, of every tree; You *are* Existence in which all things appear merely to reflect back You.

forty-seven

WHAT APPEARS to you as an obstacle is there to help you listen. Do not undertake any action unless you are inwardly clear. To be clear is to be without thought. The non-thinking heart knows beyond knowing what is to be done. Your job is merely to listen and so intuit Your own guidance. Do not muddy your path with unnecessary activity. Keep it simple. Your focus is on your Self. This does not mean your desire. To have your Self as your priority does not mean focusing on your welfare, on your needs, your wishes or your hopes. This would be running ahead of your Self. This is when obstacles appear. Obstacles arise to guide your personal self back to *Awareness*-Self; they arise to turn your attention away from the object of your desire and to draw you inward, to the Heart.

We see obstacles and become angry. It feels as if Life is against us. A feeling of unfairness arises, bitterness follows, and a railing against what others may receive. As soon as such feelings appear, stop and investigate this one who is angered.

Pull back to the sense of Being so innate to you. Tune in to the Silence of your Being. Is Silence feeling angry? It may be seen that Silence is not feeling anything, but nonetheless it remains, as a backdrop to feeling, as the great Watcher of feeling. The Silence-I, the Watcher-I: *Awareness-I*.

So, if I say 'I am angry', am I describing the permanent condition of I, or rather that a feeling of anger is occurring within Awareness-I? This deeper I of Awareness is beyond feeling; it is the silent witness to all your experience, *including* the one who experiences an obstacle.

An obstacle comes to return you to this I; to remind you that you are that which is prior to all movement. It comes to show you that you are prior to 'you the person', stripping you of the one who seeks, who pushes, who demands, who thinks they know what is best. It comes to draw you inward, into the Silence of Awareness-Self; into the Silence of I.

forty-eight

WHEN A being looks directly into the eyes of Love—when they themselves are looking from the Heart-eyes—they will see Pure Love, the God-Self. The eyes of the Heart transcend the personal perspective; theirs is the Impersonal view which is Compassion itself. Many feel unable to look Love so directly in the eye. It is not surprising, for Love is truly awe-inspiring; terrifying in its immensity. It is a mirror and a magnifying glass, all in one. It shows up every detail; it reveals all that has been hiding, and just as a ray of sun when shone through a magnifying glass shall burn, so the psyche-mind will burn under Love's glare. That is why, for a time, human beings feel they must avert their eyes. The Light is simply too bright, too startling. And no being can be rushed. There is a timing to being startled! The light of Love will shine in their eyes and pin them down when the time is good and right.

And when that time comes and a being looks directly into the eyes of Love—when they themselves are looking from the

Heart-eyes—they will see Pure Love, the God-Self. This is what can be called direct communion with your Self. In the experience of Self-communion, the mind is consumed by the Heart. Misunderstanding is absorbed; layers are seen; melting begins; and Unconditional Love is experienced as your own nature. Tears fall and confirm that what is felt is true. When Love recognises Itself it cannot help but cry tears of relief, of joy, of recognition, of release, of wonder. These tears contain everything: they contain all of your threads; all the knots of countless misunderstandings throughout countless lifetimes. In the seeing of Pure Love it is as if all those tight emotional coils are forcibly unspun. Suddenly you find yourself crying for all of it, for all that you have believed yourself to be, and for that which you now discover yourself to be. These tears are tremendous, so let them come. Even when you don't know what you are crying for, keep crying. Tears bring you to your knees and to the most sacred condition of all—humility.

The thinking mind cannot possibly comprehend the house of light that it is. But each new piece of the psyche that is unravelled and released through holy tears is brightening the Light that you are.

forty-nine

THE THINKING mind craves to be understood; it craves recognition, approbation, praise and gratitude. It is very painful to the thinking mind to be unacknowledged. The question often asked is: why would I do anything unless there is some kind of return? A return can be something as simple as a thank you. But to be reliant on a return is the definition of suffering. Are you doing so that someone else must respond, or are you doing for your Self? Expectation pulls you out of this moment and into an anticipated future. The seeker of reward has a never-ending job. For the minute you receive reward you will be hungry for more. So, who is this one who is craving praise, who seeks to do only for gain?

The seeker of reward is the seeker of love. The one who craves to be understood is the seeker of love. The mind seeks both reward and understanding as confirmation of its existence. The mind stands on shaky ground, because it does not know its true reality. And so it looks to the world for both completion and confirmation in an effort to give itself a firm base. But neither are ever realised, which only compounds the mind's feeling of being alone and unstable. You will never be understood, you will never receive enough thanks or praise or congratulation. This desire is a bottomless pot, and the effort to fill it will exhaust you.

If all action is done for its own sake—for love, by love, through love, *as Love*—then what need could there be for reward? You may do and receive nothing in return for your effort. But is it really nothing? The reward of knowing that you are not the Doer is beyond calculation. It is peace itself. Can you renounce the one who thinks they are doing? Can you prostrate yourself, hands at the feet of That, and surrender your existence to Existence? Who is it who allows you to breathe, to think, to talk, to move? It is because of That that you exist in this form. In time you shall know that you *are* That. But first you must allow yourself to be devoured. Love, Light, Existence, God, whatever your word is for the Doer, know that only by allowing yourself to be swallowed by Love shall you then shine as the Light that you are.

fifty

I HAVE come to devour you. First, I will take your head: all your thoughts, your ideas, your memories, your opinions, your dreams, your desires, your likes, your dislikes. To struggle is only to make the process more painful. There is nothing to do but surrender yourself and trust that I shall take all. Next, I shall take your hands. These hands have believed themselves to be holding the reins of this life; they consider that they are in control and that their effort makes them the doer. Who are you without head and without hands? Who are you without thinking and without doer-ship? Next, I will take your heart. I will take your emotional heart that has so far been defining this you, and then I will take the intuitive heart. Yes, even the intuitive heart. Even this heart is not the essential you. Intuition may come, but your attachment to it and your desire to bring it into expression arises out of a personal view. Head, hands, heart, and now the rest of you. Not a speck of form shall remain. As you watch yourself being devoured, what is your discovery? What might be left with all of you gone?

What remains is Love. Now I experience my own omnipresence. I am appearing as a body with a name; I am appearing as the sofa, as the table, as the structure of this room. I am appearing as people, as words, as sunshine, as poverty, as hatred, as war, as struggle, as wealth, as nature, as technology, as prayer, as cars, as pollution, as worms, as birds, as every living thing. I am appearing as the sky and the celestial bodies that sit in that sky. I am appearing as money, as faith, as faithlessness, as understanding and as misunderstanding. I am appearing as infants, as children, as adults, as the aged; I am appearing as memory of loved ones and of past experiences, as premonition of future experiences. I am the cloud that talked with me; I am the bumblebee that pointed the way; I am the song on the radio that sung my very own words. That is why I could speak their language, for I see that it is my language. I knew them so intimately because I *am* them. I am not separate from any appearance. In everything I see my Self. And this one who sees even my Self? This one who is realising the Love that I am in all its wondrous forms? If I am there witnessing my own omnipresence, then who could *I* be?

Now I am devoured. Here no words shall find Me.

fifty-one

THE MORE I surrender to the I Am that I Am, and the more the body/mind becomes a pure mirror to and an expression of the I am that I Am, the more I discover the sweetest, most intimate treasure—that this I too is very subtly phenomenal. I find myself asking: so who is this I who is seeing the I am that I am? *Who is watching the Watcher?* Is there something prior even to my own Awareness, to Beingness? Such a sincere question is its very own answer. If I am there witnessing both Self *and* the thinking mind, then I am beyond both the I-me and the I-Self. I am that out of which even Consciousness was born. Now I may see the Trinity of I: the I that gave birth to the I of Consciousness, which in turn gave birth to the I of a person.

So, why would this deepest I need to give birth to the I of Consciousness? My own immersion in my sense of Existence reveals the answer. I have no limit. And if I have no limit then I am eternally so; I am one with myself. What is one with itself cannot see itself. It needs a mirror. I gave birth to the great emanation of light-energy called Consciousness so that I might witness I. And in turn this mighty mirror of Consciousness gave birth to billions of light-mirrors, each with their inherent capacity to shine a pure image of I back to I.

This is why the mirror that is the personal you must be clear. Lifetimes of identification as a body/mind have created cloudiness upon the mirror. The vision cannot help but get caught up in the cloudiness. The mind believes that the cloudiness is the reality because it cannot imagine anything other than what it immediately sees. Nothing is wrong, as such. Cloudiness is your unique and divine 'obstruction', a beautiful and timely display, helping you to uncover the Eternal You. But it takes earnest and sincere cleaning of this mirror to see such benevolence, and to see the beauty and precision even in limitation.

Once the mirror is cleared of obstruction, what is seen? A pure image of your Self is now seen. The I of the person is a mirror to the I of Consciousness, which is Itself a mirror to the I beyond. But consider this image, is it not a *reflection*? A reflection may be now pure and untrammelled, but it is nonetheless *still a reflection*. A reflection has no substance, it is a mirage. If Consciousness is the mirror through which a deeper I may shine, then each of us as reflections of the deeper I are but facsimiles of this deeper Reality. There is no language to explain this deeper I, but in the purifying of your mind you shall at last have a glimpse of I. And the only way in which you might purify your mind, or clarify that cloudiness, is to jump into the knowing that you know beyond all—into the Silence of I.

fifty-two

THERE IS no mother, no father, no brother, no sister; there is no husband, no wife, no child—at least not in the way you have so far understood. There is no one here to support you; there is only You. To be pushed beyond what you think you know causes great fear. Fear arises out of dependence on form. Fear arises because you still think yourself to be a person distinct from other persons. This distinction keeps you feeling isolated and separate, which in turn feeds the dependence on form—your own and other forms—to sustain you. But this person who you are residing as is temporary and inconsistent; it cannot be relied upon. Everything about it changes in every moment. The physical being you are now is not the physical being you were yesterday. The emotional being you are now is not the emotional being you will be tomorrow. To rely on the form to sustain you is to be in a position of constant instability. So, how to transcend dependence on form and the need of support? How to know true Self-reliance?

Put your hand on the centre of your chest and see if you can tune in to the space under your palm. Allow your focus to settle here. Feel the expansiveness of this space. Does it stop at the edges of your palm; can you put an outline around space? Be this expansiveness, this space that has no edges. Now you are tuning in to the You that is not your body, but is still you. Does this space-like you change in any way? When you look and see, is space ever not there?

Consciousness expresses its own reality in so many beautiful ways. Think of a film reel as it is projected onto a movie screen. Each frame has its moment and it passes; the impermanent within the Permanent. What a perfect way of getting our attention! You *are* the movie screen on which the film reel runs. You are likewise a character on your own movie screen. You will come and you will go within You. Mother, father, sister, brother are likewise players in this great plot. They, too, will come and go within You. This You speaks as You in every living thing. This You is beyond conception. This You has no beginning, no end; it cannot come and it cannot go. You cannot circumscribe this You. This You is the infinite Heart of Being. This You is Consciousness-Awareness itself. To reside in conscious awareness of Yourself is to be without need and without fear. To be Self-reliant is to have given yourself wholly to the wisdom of your Self; to the unchanging, unending space of You.

fifty-three

TO STEP into the Heart is to free-fall. The mind says, but I don't want to fall, I want to fly. The mind feels that falling equates with failure, with losing, with stupidity, with uncertainty, with depression, with death. To free-fall is to surrender control. This is terrifying to the mind. It thinks that to let go of control is to give up on life. It wants to be certain of outcomes, have provisions in place; it wants to be clear of its destination and to have a plan for what it will do when it gets there. The mind considers planning essential to its well-being, for to plan is to think oneself in control. In wanting to fly as opposed to free-falling, the mind is poetically claiming its right to be an individual. It is asserting its capacity to know what is best for itself. It has decided that happiness equates with steering its own ship, flying its own plane. But this pilot is stealing your creativity. This pilot is luring you into a false sense of security because it is terrified of losing control.

To free-fall is to step into the Heart. It is innate trust that you will be caught. It is a collapsing of the thinking mind into that which knows nothing. To free-fall is to step into the unknown and into the Unknown. The relative unknown is that which is unplanned, unforeseen, unregulated, unanticipated, unexpected; it is spontaneous, undemanding, free of desire, free of want; it is without control of any kind because it is without fear. To step into the unknown is to know beyond knowing that the One who guides knows precisely which path you are here to tread. By surrendering what you think you desire, what is yours in this life becomes abundantly and effortlessly clear. To plan is to hurry your path. The mind interprets this activity as positive effort, but this in fact is an abandonment of trust. Effort shall come the moment you stop planning; effort that is pure of its own self.

To fall into the *Un*known is what allows you to fall into the unknown. This is what you have come to do—to free-fall into the Heart of Pure Being until there is no one left to jump, to trust, to surrender; until there is only You, neither divisible nor indivisible, neither free nor un-free, neither real nor unreal. Simply You.

fifty-four

TO BE beyond time is not to push time. To know that you are timeless, formless, undifferentiated Awareness is to know that time knows precisely when to bloom and when to recede within relative existence. It is a seeming paradox that to know oneself to be beyond time is to be one with time. To push is to run ahead of yourself. The Timelessness of You is without the concept of time and yet, when you know this You, intuitively you shall know when effort should occur. This is the pure state of being human. Once we assume form we join the other waves within cause and effect. But to remember your origin is to flow with the current, not against it; it is to reside in permanent recognition of Your Timelessness. In this way, you will come to know of the timeliness of manifestation, without ever being caught in the thinking mind's wheel.

The minute we come into human form we forget Timelessness, and find ourselves locked in the clock of this world. Days and activities are organised accordingly. We measure effort with our concept of time, we measure worth by our concept of time; we even measure ourselves by our concept of time. 'I am this person who is this age. I have a limited amount of time before I die and therefore must organise all activity into this limited time.' No wonder we rush, no wonder we panic, for the mind is in a constant race against time, against what we perceive as death. To consider yourself to be only the body and the mind is to feel that you are finite, which keeps you trapped in the concept of time. This is the human journey—to recognise the One who is turning this wheel, to see that the finite is an aspect within the infinite You. In this way, perfect timing may be free to unfold in the Timelessness of You.

fifty-five

A LIFE of thinking and believing is a life behind clouds. To think is to abdicate trust. It is to go ahead of your Self. To believe is to commit yourself to ideas that are continuously subject to change. To live truly is not to think, not to believe in anything. Can you in this moment allow yourself to be completely stupid? It may seem a silly suggestion, but truly, to be completely stupid is to know Real Intelligence. Feel the space that comes when you allow the possibility of not having any answers about anything. Notice the contraction that comes when you try to hold on to answers and ideas. To hold on to an idea is like trying to squeeze an ocean into a narrow canal. It is tight beyond tight. What extraordinary relief in the acceptance that you don't have answers. This shall lead you to Real Intelligence, for to know Real Intelligence is to know beyond knowing that you know no-*thing*. To know no-*thing* is to know beyond knowing that you are beyond thought, beyond belief, beyond all things. It is to know that you are the Formlessness in which all forms appear.

The mind says, but of course I must think. How will I function otherwise? How will I work, how will I pay the bills, how will I feed my children? But, my beloved, who is this One who is eternally feeding you? Hand over responsibility to the One who feeds all and see if you become in any way irresponsible. You will do your duty and better than you have ever done it before, for there shall be no thinker getting in the way, thinking and worrying which action is best. The wisdom of Being contains the wisdom of the visible universe. There is no need to search outside of yourself for answers. All is contained within You.

Put your hand on your chest and tune in to the Silence of your Being, to the You that is not your body but is still you. Be the You that is *observing* your body; the You that is eternally watching your thinking mind—the You of Awareness itself. The more you reside as Awareness-You, the more the thinking aspect will loosen its ties. Thoughts need not be your nemesis; merely your commitment to thoughts keeps your view limited. From the perspective of the *Eternal Observer* thoughts will still come, but their flavour will be different. They will not be sticky with opinion or judgement; they shall be fresh, spontaneous and broad of view. Be as the sky that is behind the clouds. What a vista there shall be! Action will flow unimpeded, whilst You witness this theatre of Your creation.

fifty-six

THE DEEPER you plunge into the Ocean of You the wider the ripples shall spread. To plunge is to recognise; it is to remember that you *are* the Ocean. We know that part of the human journey is to become momentarily mesmerised by our personal wave, by the one who constitutes a me. During this period, we forget that our wave cannot exist autonomously, that it has no life of its own without its parent, the Ocean. As soon as we forget the Parent, we begin to hold on to form; we look to form to replace the Parent, to fill us with the love that now feels missing. Form will appear as an experience, as a person, as a material object. But nothing of form will last. All *things* end. And so a human being suffers, because whatever they have been holding on to will at some point leave or change. Expression cannot repeat itself. Each happening is unique in form. It comes to dance for a brief moment and then is gone. All experiences arise within your Awareness and then disappear back into your Awareness. You as the great wine-taster must learn to savour and then spit out!

How drunk on experience the body/mind shall become if it does not learn to spit out. The body/mind has no choice but to taste, constantly; that is the deal of coming into form. But when it has forgotten the deeper Reality, the body/mind becomes not only addicted to experience, but very demanding of the type of experience it wants. To the identified mind, experience has one purpose: to give us what we think we want. At its core, this impetus is an unconscious desire to replicate the original Parental Love. Of course, no worldly experience, person or object can replicate that. Nonetheless, the mind chases experiences that taste good, and feels tormented by those it perceives as bad. But what is understood as good and bad is relative to each person's set of expectations. And it takes a very strong and active will to try and meet those expectations; a will that cannot see the bigger picture; a will that cannot see that everything is for your good, that there is no right or wrong, no good or bad, and that there is only experience for learning.

A wave cannot move of its own volition. It requires the great body of the Ocean behind it. Nothing you do, nothing that occurs, can happen without the Parent guiding proceedings. It is because of the Parent that you breathe, that you listen, that you talk, that you work, that you love, that you cry, that you experience, that you exist. We fight to hold our head above water only because we are struggling to separate ourselves from the Ocean. But how can we separate ourselves from what we essentially are? We want to assert our right to be individual, and so will swim against the current to prove our own power, to prove that we can carve out our own experiences to match our needs. What would it be like no longer to hold your head above water? What would it be like no longer to resist the current? What would it be like to sink into the Ocean and allow yourself to be drowned? Let go of the swimmer in you. How exhausting it is to keep up momentum. We feel that to stop swimming will be to stop living; we fear to drown because we fear to lose control. Surrender this control and let You the Ocean swim you the person, effortlessly, beautifully, uniquely as you.

fifty-seven

YOU ARE here to cultivate the Real Relationship, the one with your own beloved Self. All human beings are searching for love. Every action and impulse in this world is a demonstration of this search. This search is a holy search, for at its heart lies a knowing that happiness is the realisation of love. But, in the early stages of our evolution, the understanding of love is *personal* and relative. Our dependence on loved ones to fulfil our needs fills every chapter of our lives. We look to the child, to the mother, to the husband, to the girlfriend to complete us. But no matter the beauty of each relationship, there will still remain a feeling of lack, a feeling that something is missing, and an underlying sense of loneliness.

The moment we became committed to being a body/mind was the moment we felt separate from all other body/minds. This is the root of loneliness. Because we consider ourselves to be alone and disconnected, we then seek to fill an apparent void. Within that 'void' is true remembrance of completion in love. And so, our first taste of love in another person is in fact pure. Because what are you tasting? This is the recognition that you know without knowing how you know. You are tasting your Self in that other. But what happens almost instantaneously is that the personal perspective limits this love and tries to contain it. For as long as humans feel finite, we shall hold on to happiness in whatever form it appears, and will be terrified at the prospect of loss. The other person becomes the sole container of love, and without that other, we shall feel bereft, alone, without love.

This does not make relationship wrong; quite the contrary, it is a gift. For it is through relationship that you may come to let go of relationship. Is it not the case that your capacity to love is constantly being tested? No one will hit your buttons quite as strongly as someone you care for. This makes each of your loved ones your greatest teacher, because through each button you are being asked to face the details of your personal self. These details are blocking your true understanding of yourself, and so by looking with tender and compassionate precision at each button that is hit, you will slowly unravel yourself of all limitation. The falling in love with an 'other' is a divine stepping stone towards falling in love with your own Self. Because the question will come: who is this one who is so dependent on another for my happiness? And is it truly me? The moment will come when you are pushed off the precipice into Real Love. When it is tasted there is no going back, and yet, that does not mean that personal relationship may not be enjoyed.

Within Love of Self relative love will emerge, and most beautifully, for it will be without need and without demand. It shall be without projection and without expectation. We shall no longer define ourselves by our relationships. We shall no longer depend upon an 'other' for confirmation of our existence. There shall no longer be an 'other'. You shall see your own Self as every living being, as every form. What *need* could there be for relationship when it is seen that that which is being related to is none other than your own Self? Now you may truly be as you are with all forms of You; this is the freedom of Real Love.

fifty-eight

T HE ONE who avoids relationship is equal in weight to the one who chases it. The human emotional heart is a complex and highly sensitive mechanism. It is the gateway, if you like, to the Pure Heart of Being. But, very easily, this gateway can become guarded, its key refusing to be unlocked. Sometimes, great boulders of pain grow in front of those gates, refusing entry to all. It will not concede even one chink of light, because the light feels even more painful than what is being held behind that gateway.

What is pain? The original pain is the pain of separation, the pain of having forgotten the Self. The roots of our collective human conditioning begin with this deep feeling of loss. As a consequence of feeling separate and isolated, human beings automatically feel vulnerable and in need. Out of this fundamental misunderstanding walls of self-protection are built. And this finds expression in the personal story. Every time a personal need is not met, every time we feel isolated and afraid, another layer of pain is added to that wall, and the emotional heart receives further confirmation that Love is not to be trusted. After all, did Love not let us down? Did the original Parent not abandon us? This is not conscious as such, but nonetheless the personal story will reflect this root misunderstanding. Mother, father, husband, wife, all 'others' shall let us down at some point and deny us the love we feel we need. The sense of betrayal and the sense of abandonment are so primary to the psyche, so raw, that many hearts simply feel they cannot risk further hurt. And so, those walls grow deeper and more unyielding.

Pain is a misunderstanding of yourself. This *is* the boulder at the gateway that protects your emotional heart. And this is what becomes the personal identity. Human beings believe that their emotional world is the core of who they are. We hold on to our pain and define ourselves with our pain: 'I am the person who this happened to; I am the one who has suffered like this.' Pain thus becomes our shield; we try to protect ourselves from pain with our shield of pain. But this shield silences the heart; it will not allow you to feel *truly*. And so, one expression of the original feeling of separation is an active *denial* of relationship, an active denial of love. What a twist in this drama that we should put up walls against the very thing we crave. And yet, entirely understandable; for it is true that the Light that threatens to pierce through this boulder is more terrifying, more startling, than anything the mind could conceive. There is nothing more frightening to the mind than the realisation of Pure Love. Because in that recognition all that has been held in place must tumble, brick by brick, layer by layer, until nothing is left of this one you call you.

fifty-nine

TO BE rooted as You is to flower as you. You cannot
fully know who you are *in* manifestation until you
know who you are *beyond* manifestation. And you cannot
fully stabilise in who you are beyond form until you know
who you are in form. In other words, awakening to the
Reality of You is but the first step. From here, from this
deeper wisdom, the personality may be raked through. Not
a coal may be left unturned. This is where the mind can
jump in and assume that the story is unimportant. Your
story is the aspect within Truth that has become limited,
curtailed, circumscribed; which makes looking at it all the
more important. It is all You; merely the personality-you
has become locked behind walls. By understanding the story
you break down these walls and thus see that there is no
separation between boundless-You and form-you. *It is all
You.* Your story is your unique path, written with benevolent
precision, as a tool-kit for coming Home. Those first steps
shall be the most auspicious, for once you have begun this

unravelling, there shall be no stopping until there is no one left to unravel.

It is not tiring or even overwhelming. Life proceeds with infinite caution, infinite care, laying before you what is needed to be faced at just the right moment. There is nothing to do but offer yourself up for dissection. The mind shall hurt; it shall try to slip out from under Love's knife. But, place it back, firmly. It shall be seen that even this pain is part of a joyous disenfranchisement of everything you thought yourself to be. Pain arises only from misunderstanding. So, face each misunderstanding; face the one who feels tired at the prospect of self-observation, the one who is overwhelmed or hurt. If you hurt know that the one who is hurt is ready to be investigated. Go to this, lay it out on the table, dissect its attributes, each nuance; understand what makes it tick and what makes it grow; look to the details of your story to see where the seeds were first sown. But all the while, even in the midst of the strongest pain, keep bringing your focus back to the eyes of the Heart and look from there.

Such enquiry can only be of benefit if the scalpel of dissection is lovingly detached from the object of enquiry. To look with compassion from a meaningful distance shall allow you to understand truly. To look without judgement, without anger, recrimination or fear is to look from the deeper wisdom of I. This is available to you as your Conscience. Your Conscience knows each note of your story; each subtle cadence is compassionately seen, compassionately understood. And so you will know the Perfection of your story; a divine play, come to remind you of You. This is how each flower in existence shall bloom, once rooted in the Heart of Self-knowledge.

sixty

WHO ARE you? Are you the person with this kind of temperament? Are you the person who likes this kind of food; who is attracted to this type of person; who works at this job; who wishes to be doing something else in life? Are you the person who loves to hike, to dance, to play football, to sing, to paint, to read, to go on adventures? So many aspects, so many you's. How many you's are you? In different company we become a different kind of you. With this person we are this kind of you; with another we have quite opposite attributes; at work we display another form of you; with each member of our family we are an altered type of you. To believe whole-heartedly in ourselves as a person is to plug unconsciously into each change. This is why this friend knows you as this kind of a person and another as a totally different kind of a person. But, where in all that you-ness are *you*?

To find out who you are, first know that all you think yourself to be is not fundamentally you. The details of the personality are the unique flavours, but first we must discover the base upon which they may be savoured. Close your eyes and see if you can find you. Tune in to that intimate, innate sense of yourself. The *sense* of oneself is without form or shape. This is the you who cannot be seen, who cannot be touched. In the looking for you it is suddenly revealed that you are without attribute. You just Are. To reside as You Are is to know beyond knowing that You are beyond the flavour of your personality and yet, at the same time, You contain all those beautiful details. But as long as those flavours remain strong they will dominate and determine your view. The flavours are not wrong; simply they do not contain the whole picture. As soon as you begin to taste the deeper picture of I, you shall be in the prime position to investigate the little I. Now you are safe to enter the psyche-cave.

Each being must enter the cave of their own psyche and face all that is in there. This is a very holy cave to enter, for what priceless treasure shall be found within—your very own heart. But first you must face all that lurks in the shadows of this cave. This is each hero and heroine's journey: to face the monsters of misunderstanding. There is no escape route, no alternative path, no avoiding these monsters. They must be confronted, head on, with all the love and compassion of the Pure Heart. The only way of safely dissecting is to look from the eyes of the Heart, and the only way to stabilise in the Heart is to dissect those attributes of the psyche that have become limited. Both must happen simultaneously in order that you may bring misunderstanding into understanding and so reach for that most precious of all pearls—Self-knowledge. Now, and only now, shall the individual-you shine, as the changeable aspect within the unchanging You.

sixty-one

MANY BEINGS feel confused at this moment of the journey. Words come, such as: never in my life have I felt so identified as a me. And for a period of time this is true. When we take our first steps into the Light of Love, all the personality traits momentarily burn. Your buttons will never feel so hit; issues that you had thought were long buried suddenly rise up and shout at you, unremittingly. It is as if your personal story were writ in large neon letters across your forehead for all the world to see. Never have you felt so exposed, so vulnerable, so terrifyingly raw. Your emotions will be red to the bone with sensitivity, and reactivity will reach its height. But all is well. Imagine a dark cellar that for many years has been locked and hidden away from the light. One day you open a door on that cellar and replace the broken bulb. Suddenly everything is exposed; all the dust, dirt and debris of lifetimes are now under the glare of light. Darkness is merely an absence of light. Brighten the space and, quite simply, nothing can escape.

Coming to the Heart is a messy and turbulent affair.

Allow it to be; allow it to be noisy and uncomfortable. Allow yourself to be spilled out all over the floor; let Love take you into the deepest shadows of your psychology, into all the layers that make up this me. There are layers inside of your layers. You are an intricate and complex creation, so this is not going to happen overnight. But there is only one way of safely walking into the psyche-cave and that is to hold on to your torchlight—to keep your focus on that knowing that you know without knowing how you know, on Love. Put yourself in Love's hands and know that you will be peeled, gently, firmly and consistently. The minute one layer is exposed another will materialise. In this way, you will come to know each tendency of your mind. By facing each tendency with clarity and discernment, you will begin to feel learned patterns loosen their grip. Love will keep digging; it will test you constantly, so that all that is in limitation can be seen through.

But have patience. The human mind wants everything now; it craves immediacy and wants sensory proof that it has achieved something. Even a direct and immediate Seeing shall be followed by a painstaking peeling of layers. So, do not hurry. The mind is quick to judge itself. It says: I wish I wasn't like this; I wish my mind would go away and leave me in peace. The initial wish for change is sincere, but so quickly the mind jumps in and pushes for resolution. Love knows what it is doing, and there is a timing to your evolution. All that is required is a sincere heart. All shall be revealed to the sincere heart. The sincere heart does not flicker and flit from one thing to another. The sincere heart is focused on Truth alone. The sincere heart knows that it is under Love's microscope; and as soon as distraction comes, it knows to put itself back under.

126

∞ sixty-two ∞

COLLECTIVE TURBULENCE is a reflection of the inner turbulence of the mind; it is an external expression of misunderstanding. The original misunderstanding is the forgetting of the Self: the belief that I am other to you. This then grows into personalised misunderstanding between those I's and you's. Humans experience misunderstanding as emotional or physical pain. Each being has their own language of misunderstanding; their own unique pair of emotional spectacles through which they view the world. This view can only ever be limited for it can only ever appreciate a certain perspective. Every interaction, every response that comes from the thinking mind will only ever be limited, and will therefore cause turbulence. One set of spectacles comes up against another set of spectacles, each with their own way of seeing, and neither can understand the other. Reactivity occurs, energy overspills itself and the vibration of discontent ripples outwards. Every thought, word, deed or action leaves its imprint. Every identified thought creates and leaves behind it a dissonant sound. This sound reverberates throughout Creation and feeds Creation, for it is not separate from Creation. All that emerges from the *non*-identified mind *resonates* throughout Creation. All dissonance desires to return to resonance. All discord desires to return to harmony. All darkness is craving the light. Darkness is not the opposite to the Light; it is simply the absence of recognition of the Light; a misunderstanding of the Self.

You are Light, Sound and Vibration. To come into recognition of this great emanation that is Consciousness—the godly current—is the definition of peace. To know yourself to *be* the current is the definition of peace. Turbulence arises when we forget the current of our being. From tsunami to war, from earthquake to epidemic, all such phenomena arise out of misunderstanding in the thinking mind. The thinking mind *is* the collective mind. Therefore, your duty is to purify *your* mind. This is how you 'help the world'. For none of that exists without You; none of that occurs without your permission. We look outwards to the world and wish to change it. This movement itself is an act of misunderstanding. The world will change only once you have changed yourself; once you have turned that spotlight inward and asked: to whom is this turbulence occurring? Who is this one who suffers? Who is this one who feels pain? And is it the essential me?

Only then may the Divine Note chime as you, may you resonate as the One Vibration, may you shine as the Light that you are.

sixty-three

THERE IS nothing more important than knowing Happiness. Fears arise and argue that there is no time to be happy: there is work to do, chores to be done, responsibilities to attend to. But, Happiness does not lie outside of these activities. Another voice says, but I have to live in the 'real world'. In discovering Happiness you will recognise that you do not live in the world, the world lives in You. All your previous duties will be done and better than before, for there will be no attachment to outcome, no worry of failure, no pushing and striving and wishing things to be otherwise. There will be no pusher full stop. The one who pushes runs ahead of Happiness. To know Happiness is to allow without demanding, to give effort effortlessly, to neither seek to know nor seek to gain; it is recognition that Happiness merely Is.

Every thought, every impulse, every movement, every action is an appearance within Consciousness and shall therefore have an effect in Consciousness. Each wave causes a ripple effect. This is unavoidable. An impulse of misunderstanding will reverberate within itself. These reverberations shall be felt within Consciousness; they cannot be separated from the 'rest' of Consciousness. It is not that a misunderstanding is felt only by the person feeling it. Everything is Consciousness; therefore, one ripple is felt by the entirety. It may be said, well, one tiny wave has no impact on the immensity of the ocean. What happens when seven billion waves are each creating similar ripples? Shall they not create a great turbulence within the ocean; shall they not accumulate into a collective tsunami? This is the level of responsibility we each have towards happiness; to discover Happiness is nothing less than your duty.

Happiness is that in which all things happen. It has no preference, no likes or dislikes, no wants or needs; it merely Is. You can discover Happiness right now by turning the spotlight inward. Who is aware of this person called 'you'? Who is eternally present no matter what mood you are in? Who is silently watching whatever experience is in front of you? I am. This I cannot be touched or seen. This I is formless, limitless, like space. The most I can say is that I am like a vast silence. I am neither breathing nor not breathing, neither seeing nor not seeing, neither hearing nor not hearing. But I am aware of the one who is breathing, seeing, hearing. I am the Awareness of all things. The form of I appears within this formless I. *All* ripples appear within I. I am not separate from the ripples because I am made of the same stuff. What unending happiness is this discovery: that I am the Stuff of Happiness itself.

sixty-four

IF YOU want to be happy you have to be willing to disagree with yourself on every point. You must be willing to be wrong about everything. You must be willing to go back to babyhood and learn from a blank slate. This baby will cry for a while; it will feel pain and it will want to return to what it thinks it knows. All that you have accumulated throughout this lifetime is up for inspection, and it is time now to un-swaddle yourself. But, it is not a trial. No matter how painful to the mind, this fine-sifting shall become your joy. Why? Because the divine Inspector is Compassion itself. This Inspector has no judgement. To give yourself to this Inspector is to know that all that has accumulated has been for your own good; it is to bare your back to the rod of Love and to know that this rod will undo you of all misunderstanding. Everything that you perceive to have happened to you is for your own good, especially when it hurts.

If you want to be happy, you must be willing to experience hurt. The human mind is full of investments. To be divested of investments is very painful to the mind. The mind wants to hold on to its bounty in the form of its thought processes, its memories, its feelings and experiences. It thinks that this is the treasure that will bring happiness; it thinks that this treasure will bring love. Real Love will pull the plug wherever investment is found throughout all manifestation. Can you therefore say thank you for each stroke, knowing that it has come to free the one who has buried itself in layers of investment; to free the one who can feel hurt. Is the Silence of You feeling hurt? Is the Silence of You ever hurt? Look now and see. This enquiry shall dig so deep that you will come to see there is no-*thing* happening to you. It is only the *person* who feels something is happening *to* them, for they feel separate from all things, and therefore at the mercy of all things.

If you want to be happy you have to be willing. Without willingness your mind shall construct an ever denser wall around your heart. Willingness for Truth is the first step. It is the step to breach that wall. What an auspicious rupture! Can you see now the benevolence of Love? For in the stripping of all investment you shall come to Nothing. Willingness, openness and sincerity. Lay those at Love's feet and know that the divine dismantling has begun.

sixty-five

THE MIND wants to feel strong and confident. It is quick to feel undermined by someone else or by a situation. Strategies are learned to help maintain self-confidence, and to uphold a feeling of strength. But these strategies can only ever give a superficial and temporary sense of strength. They are dependent on so many things: on your mood, on the circumstances. In the deepest part of us we know Real Strength, but without true Self-Confidence it cannot be expressed. We often, for example, find ourselves in a situation which we know is not truthful; the heart speaks a clear but silent 'no', but the mind has not yet learned how to articulate that 'no' purely. There are two alternatives to this mind: either to sink in silence and not speak up, or to charge in and criticise. Both will diminish you; both will leave you feeling deeply uncomfortable with yourself; neither will express Real Strength. Questions come, such as: but what of someone who experiences violence? Surely it is natural to react and demonstrate strength when under threat?

Imagine a little boy who for years has been beaten by his father. The beating has stripped him of his voice, his confidence and his strength. Then, one day, when he has reached his adolescence, his father reaches out to hit him once more and the young man suddenly lashes back. With all his might he pushes his father back and onto the floor. His body and mind shake with the shock of his outburst; he is flooded with a mix of relief, fear and excitement. He feels for the first time the flame of self-confidence flickering into existence. The father too is silenced by the reaction. This was the boy's first 'no'.

The reactive no will always be messy and turbulent, but that does not make it wrong. It is the first step towards a deeper response. The Conscience is ever present. You know what is good and true without knowing how you know. Simply, you are not yet stable in your Conscience; not yet fully Self-Confident. Really to feel what is good and pure is to stand as You Are, to stand in the Heart. It is to listen to the Silence of your Being. What emerges from this deepest listening is Real Strength, your innate wisdom, your Conscience. And sometimes the Conscience is very firm indeed. *Love is also no.* Love will not concede any dishonesty. It knows what to do, when to do, if to do, how to do; but it is never reactive. It sees misunderstanding in another, but understands with full compassion why such behaviour should develop. This means it is never in judgement. The emotional heart will fight for its personal space, while the Pure Heart sees with clarity and discernment.

Your task is to stand in your knowing of what is right and good. From now on let not one word or deed come from you that does not come from the Conscience. How does it feel if you let Love talk through you? Stand before your loved ones as Love, and see what words come. You could not possibly anticipate what will come, for Heart is eternally spontaneous. Only know that whatever comes from the Pure Heart will never hurt anyone, no matter how much the mind may feel hurt. Love is a sword that cuts through to truth; that is the definition of Real Strength. And the one who resides as the Love that they are is the one who is fully Self-Confident.

✑ sixty-six ✑

WHY DO people do things to hurt other people? Why must some beings receive strong treatment at the hands of others? The mind's position is to judge. It is quick to decide that someone is bad, or that someone else has done an evil thing; that 'wrong-doers' must be punished. It is true that each being will have to face the roots and the consequences of their actions, but facing oneself is not the same as judging oneself. When the thinking mind stands in judgement of another thinking mind it is equivalent to a medical student attempting to perform heart surgery on his first day of training. The student has not yet learned basic anatomy; he knows nothing of the entire workings of the body, and is just learning how to hold a scalpel correctly. To place him in charge of such a delicate procedure would be very dangerous indeed. He simply does not have the scope of vision yet.

The thinking mind lives in a world of opposites. It is very literal in its understanding and sees things in a very black and white way. It is quick to define roles and highlight a victim in opposition to a perpetrator. To designate a victim and a perpetrator is a contraction of seeing. It solidifies the belief that I am separate from you: that we are at the mercy of outside forces. A victim is permanently under attack from outside forces, and a perpetrator is in a continual state of trying to control outside forces, because at root, they too feel under attack. Both aspects are a profound misunderstanding of the reality. Who is the one who feels under attack? This one is the thinking mind who feels separate, isolated and alone, like an island that is under threat of invasion.

Whenever you encounter strong behaviour in yourself or in another, bring your focus to the eyes in the centre of the chest. Look at the behaviour from these eyes. These eyes have a panoramic scope. In their innate compassion and discernment they understand all the details of behaviour. From this perspective, there is no such thing as something bad; there is only misunderstanding, and therefore there is always an opportunity for learning. Heart surgery is the most subtle of all investigations. It cannot be undertaken with literal eyes. Learn to look in the abstract, to read between the lines of each being, and then you will understand the delicate workings of all.

∽ sixty-seven ∽

CRITICISM CARRIES a very bad smell. It poisons the air. It poisons the one who has been critical and leaves its trace long after it is expressed. Every vibration of criticism is a vibration of dissonance. Every time a negative or demeaning thought or word is uttered about another person that dissonant sound adds to the collective dissonance. Your comment of impatience or irritation is not isolated. It is creating hurricanes of confusion, a cauldron of hatred, a war between so many worlds. Your mind has so far been your world. It comes up against another world, and from its position of isolation, it has no compass, no way of navigating this unknown terrain. And what the mind doesn't understand it doubts, derides, castigates. The mind will always *think* it has good reason to be critical: 'He is so manipulative; she is so controlling; he is so stupid; she is so thoughtless.' The mind will console itself in finding everything around it wrong and unacceptable, because nothing matches up to its expectations. It feels further confirmed of its own authority; further convinced of its righteousness. But this is not righteous behaviour; this is behaviour born of misunderstanding; it is behaviour born of the mind that is consumed by its thoughts.

Criticism forms the thinking base of every identified mind. This mind has no choice but to be in a state of criticism because it has its own limited position to maintain. Its narrow view cannot see the bigger picture; it has no space to ask why a situation may be unfolding in a certain way. It knows only that its needs have not been met. And so, it finds itself eternally disappointed with the world. Only the one who is not yet Self-sufficient looks outwards for someone or something to meet expectations. And of course it is a fruitless search. But rather than face the reality of the search, the mind blames the world for its inadequacy, for failing to give what it supposedly promised. For this is the key: the mind feels it has been promised something; it is waiting for the moment when everything will suddenly make sense. Until everything makes sense, everything will be criticised for not making sense.

Somewhere in that jumble is a great deal of wisdom. For you have indeed been born to 'make sense' of who you are. So use this tendency to criticise as your stepping stone inward. The next time someone causes some irritation inside you, drop your focus to the centre of your chest, and look at them from there. How does it feel when you look at every situation, at every person, at every aspect of your own person from the eyes of the Heart? You will discover that these eyes have not even the capacity to criticise, for these eyes are Compassion itself. To look through the Heart-eyes is to taste your innate sense of Existence, which is to make sense, finally, of who you really are.

≈ sixty-eight ≈

TO STAND as you are is to be willing to receive much criticism. When a being begins the journey to the Heart, a very great monster is unleashed. This is the monster of doubt. It may feel as if doubt is coming at you from all angles. The moment you begin to taste the truth of your reality, your doubting mind will rise up and shout at you wherever it can. It will express itself through your loved ones. They will feel a change in you, and they may be concerned at what they see as instability. You will not be able to deny it, for it is true that one moment you are tasting the pure joy of a love you have never known before, and the next moment you find yourself overwhelmed with despair. What a see-saw it can feel; to the point where you begin to doubt your own seeing. You begin to wonder if those criticisms thrown at you do not contain some truth. And this only deepens the despair.

The truth is, those criticisms are your own self-criticisms. To come to the Heart is to have every stone of self-doubt thrown at you. Those stones hurt only if they contain your own doubt. Therefore, what a teaching they are. The one who feels hurt by outside criticism shall be pushed to the limit. This is likely to be happening just as all the structures of your former life are being torn down, one by one. Things you used to do easily are no longer easy; some things are simply no longer possible. As your life begins to topple around you, and you find yourself seemingly incapable, so more criticism may come; more questioning of your 'choices'. You will be shouting at yourself just as others are shouting at you wanting to know why you are doing what you are doing. But, beloved, what is happening to you cannot be explained. You can barely explain it to yourself, so how can you possibly make sense to others? Allow both your mind and your loved ones their wobble and their concern. It is necessary for their journey. Remember, there is nothing more terrifying to the thinking mind than to see another thinking mind unravel itself. And in that fear, the mind contracts into condemnation.

But all is well. This is the great gift of criticism, for it is asking you to stand as you are, to trust this fracturing of everything you call you, and to know it is for your good. You in the form of your loved ones are appearing to push you ever deeper into your knowing so that you have no choice but to say: I don't know how I know this Love, but I know it.

❧ sixty-nine ❧

NO ONE will ever be able to understand you. The one who worries about what other people think is causing you so much suffering; the one who craves other people to 'get you' is causing you so much suffering. How many times have you felt a lack of understanding even amongst your loved ones? Many beings grow up with the feeling that they somehow 'don't fit in', that they cannot find anyone who talks their own language. Standing in a room with hundreds of familiar faces can leave you feeling more alone and misunderstood than if you were entirely by yourself. Relationships end in the pain of he or she 'not understanding me'. Angry exchanges are ignited by the sharp desire to have your point of view heard and accepted. But no one will ever be able to understand you, not even if they share your point of view.

The desire to be understood is equivalent to the desire for approval. We seek approval because we are not yet comfortable with ourselves and because we are not yet residing fully as our Self. We seek to be understood because we seek to love and to be loved. All human beings are seekers of love, until they come to know the Love that they are. The seeking of love is not wrong. It is the divine spark within all beings that shall ultimately reveal who you are. Once you know who you are you will be who you are with everyone you meet. Presence shall meet Presence in every form. From this true position, the personality is then free to be its unique and idiosyncratic self. For in knowing the Self you automatically come to know the personal self. The unique mirror that is the personality-mind, having melted into its true residence, is now freed from all need, from all desire to be understood, because it is at last in full understanding of itself. Now it may sing the notes it was designed to sing, purely, effortlessly, and without discord.

The personality-mind will not melt instantaneously. There are many layers to the one who seeks to be understood. Nonetheless, now that you are coming into recognition of You, you can begin to view the little you from a compassionate distance. Allow the world to express its opinion, use whatever hurts you to unravel those layers, but all the while keep your focus on You. To reside as you are, as the Presence of Awareness, is to see with loving detachment all the aspects of the personality that are causing limitation. Therefore You are guiding you. The little you will put up a fight and demand autonomy. It will shout, 'But yes, you don't understand me. I only did this because …' Stand firm and continue to guide that little one inward. In this way, you will discover if what You are ever needs to be understood; if what You are *can* ever be understood.

❧ seventy ❧

THE THINKING mind is forever in judgement of itself. It feels unworthy of love. It feels it can never be good enough, never measure up to divine expectations. Human beings run from the very thing they crave because they feel *unworthy* of love. The feeling of being undeserving arises because the mind is quite naturally overwhelmed by the Self. The truth is that Truth is beyond all identified understanding; You are vast beyond all comprehension. In the glimpse of the Immensity, the mind recoils and feels overwhelmed by the enormity of such love. Unconditional Love feels too bright, too radiant, too terrifying in its magnitude, and so the mind turns away in fear of being swallowed up in such magnitude. The thinking mind's perception that it is alone and unprotected in this vast universe is now compounded into the condition of being unworthy, of being not good enough; of being too small, too insignificant, too unlovable to be allowed to enter such a kingdom of Love.

Imagine a child in a playground who is alone and without

friends. In their separation and isolation, the child feels that no one likes them. The assumption made by this child-mind is that if no one is with me then I must be unlovable, and undeserving of love. And here lies the root of the human feeling of rejection. After all, thinks the child-mind, if the great Parent rejected its own infant it must be because the infant is inherently undeserving. And within that pain of the 'original abandonment' are woven all the personal stories of the human psyche.

This kingdom of Love is your true ground in which to play. It is where you reside even when you are not conscious of your true residence. It is the nature of your Being. Put your hand over the centre of your chest and tune in to the Silence of your Being. Is the Silence of your Being feeling unworthy? Is the Silence of your Being feeling small and insignificant? Your task may feel herculean, but in fact it is very simple. It is to trust the knowing that you know without knowing how you know. Yes, the Love of your Being is vast beyond all conception; you are the limitless, undying Reality. You feel unworthy only because you have limited your reality to the confines of your body. So, tune in to the *essence* of you. Look now, and see if the love that emanates from the Silence of your Being can ever know a sense of unworthiness. You are more than good enough; you are Goodness itself.

seventy-one

THE COLLECTIVE psyche is full of self-hatred. It demonstrates itself in what we see as aggression and violence amongst people and nations. And in a less obvious but equally powerful way, it bleeds into each personality and therefore into all our actions and impulses. Imagine the personality like a tapestry canvas. The design has already been imprinted on the canvas; all that remains is that you follow the design with the coloured wool, bringing to life the picture that is already there. However, the wool that has come with your kit is old, frayed and faded. And your needle is far too thick and clumsy and so frequently misses or doubles up a stitch. Certain wools don't quite match the colour required on the canvas, but you use them anyway.

Your kit at birth provided you with a personality base, ready-made. You have a set of attributes that are pure and clear, but also a set of attributes that have been well worn over lifetimes. They are not in full clarity; they are your expectations, your learned tendencies, your reactive language.

They are the lessons you are here to learn. Your task is to throw out that old wool, and sew your tapestry into clean and beautiful colour, free from all former patterns, so that you may be fresh and spontaneous within your design.

To continue using old, frayed patterns is a denial of your Self. Self-hatred arises from Self-denial. All human beings will go through a period of forgetting the Self, a time of forgetting the Goodness that you are. But there comes a point when each being has to face their own culpability and take responsibility for their behaviours. And that means being willing to be wrong about everything; that means being willing to enter Love's classroom and learn afresh. Fear makes you turn away from Love's classroom, and the giving in to that fear further deepens your self-hatred. You know that the Divine Teacher will not let you get away with anything. You will have to face your anger, jealousy, blame, your desire for revenge, your greed, laziness and criticism, and see how they have fortified your stronghold of self-hatred.

But the truth is that hatred can only grow out of intense love. The love you have for the Divine Teacher is more immense than you dare to know. The moment you became confirmed as an individual person, separate and different from all others, was the moment you felt betrayed and abandoned by the Teacher. The pain of this turned the strength of your love into the pain of hatred. Therefore, the true definition of personal self-hatred is the powerful anger towards the Divine Teacher, towards the Self. What a moment you have reached, for the time for reconciliation has come. Make this your prayer: purify this one until nothing remains but the Love that I am. Because only when there is the humility to enter that classroom can your inherent nature fully shine through, and the beauty of your design be realised.

seventy-two

THE LEAVING home—the period of forgetting the Self—is all part of a human being's eventual transcendence. We have to leave home in order to return and so realise our ultimate Residence. But there is no avoiding that the behaviour that results from this forgetting can become very dense. Beings can spend years in behaviours that become denser and denser. Naturally, this has a vibrational impact. Vibrations of dissonance become compacted and tight. Like the tightly bandaged hands of a boxer and the powerful gloves on top, dissonance is armed, protected with its shield of misunderstanding and ready to fight. Underneath those gloves are the soft hands of a vulnerable child. And the more vulnerable that child feels the more it will fight, tooth and nail, to protect itself. It knows no other reality than the boxing ring, and will not engage with anyone or anything without those gloves on. All opponents take on the face of the original 'foe': the Parent who seemingly abandoned the child.

What this child does not at first realise is that Mother

allows Her children to empty their misunderstanding into violent tantrums, whilst keeping them safe and held in a firm embrace. Mother is standing in that boxing ring and receiving each vibrational impact. She holds each fighter-child as it kicks and punches, and absorbs each blow. But be assured, She will also end the rounds and say 'enough' when the fighter-child is not able to stop themselves.

Who is this Mother who can absorb all of your pain? This Mother is your very own Heart. She is the great womb of Consciousness out of which all the children of form are born. She is You. But you cannot know Mother until you put yourself in Her arms; until you allow yourself to be an infant in Her arms. The vulnerable baby will recoil; this one is your learned understanding of babyhood. This one is in defiance of Mother; it does not trust that Mother will catch it. It feels very angry and fearful of Mother, and will therefore fight Her to the end. For even when a being begins to taste Mother, the fight continues; it in fact even grows for a time. But again, this is Mother's job. She holds you in the midst of your anger; she lets every child test the boundaries, because it is through that testing that you learn. You have to burn yourself to know the strength of the fire; you have to fall so that you find yourself. This is the true definition of what some call a 'fallen angel': the pure child who has run away from home for a time and is pushing the boundaries of existence, so that you may ultimately know the Existence that you are.

⟣ seventy-three ⟢

NOTHING IS wasted; nothing is lost. No mistakes have been made. There are no failures and no successes. To know Peace is to know that everything happens for your own good; that everything happens for your learning. For even what you are calling a mistake has led you to this moment. It was what was necessary to deepen your understanding of yourself. It may seem that you are repeating 'mistakes'. If that observation has come then already wisdom is speaking. For what this really means is that a deep-rooted tendency is repeatedly exerting itself in an effort to say: 'This is me, this is who I am, this is what I need …' To see through a 'mistake' is to see through a misunderstanding, to see through the identified you. Consciousness will produce whatever means necessary so as to bring those layers of misunderstanding to your attention, to push you into relinquishing the me you think you are.

The thinking mind measures itself via its failures and successes. If some action has not borne fruit the mind considers it a waste of time, but what of the fruit of the journey? What of all that unfolded in each step? Life speaks in powerful ways. It uses your endeavours to teach you the reality—that you are not an autonomous individual; that you are not in control, determining your destiny; that you are not your ideas of success and failure; that such ideas are a personal measure of self-worth; that they keep you forever striving and never being.

What happens when you say: I don't mind? Not to mind is not to be caught up in the mind and its desires. If you were to hand over everything that you feel you want out of life, everything that you feel you are here to do, all your talents, all your gifts, all your learning, *all of you*—if you were to hand over the entire story that comprises this you and allow yourself truly not to mind what happens, what occurs within you? This you who has been holding on to an idea of you has been keeping you hostage. All the detail that is unique to this you shall be neither lost nor wasted; quite the contrary. But, it shall only be free to dance its dance once you have renounced all desire for it; once you have surrendered all desire to be a you. If you want to be happy you have no choice but to let go of the strings entirely, and thus allow You to shine as you.

seventy-four

MANY BEINGS feel their purpose in life is related to the gift of expression that comes most naturally. The poet feels they have no choice but to express in words; the dancer leaps into life with every step; the painter expresses all the colours of existence with his palette. The artist feels the collective details and gives them voice on behalf of all. To feel and dive into the complexities of the emotional heart is to pave the path towards knowing the Pure Heart. The human capacity to empathise is our stepping stone towards becoming conscious of Consciousness, because you cannot *think* Love, you can only experience it, know it, *feel* it. The deeper we feel, the more space there is for the deepest question of all—who am I? Your gift is opening the doorway into the inexpressible nature of You. For how often will an artist say that when the impetus comes, there is no choice but to write, dance, speak, sing? Simply movement comes and there is no choice but to let it flow through you into form.

At the same time, a gift brings with it a profound teaching.

The one who has a gift is likely to spend many years strongly identified as the person who can do what they can do. Such a one feels they have nothing, are nothing, without this impetus. We have heard of the artist who fears the moment when the muse is gone. Their gift becomes their reason for living, a demonstration of existence: this is who I am, this is what I do. But who are you without your gifts? For a time, many beings must be stripped of their creative capacity: a dancer whose muscles can no longer bear their weight; a singer whose throat is parched of all voice; a writer who sinks into a deep depression because no words will come to their pen.

What Grace in being stripped. Nothing is lost, quite the contrary. You are being shown who is really creating. You are being asked to hand over your form so that you may become the true instrument of the Divine. In fact, there is great wisdom in wishing the muse to stay, because in the deepest sense what the artist is really saying is, I pray that Love may continue to express through this form. The next step is to realise the human tendency to hold on to Love in the form of a gift. The agony of 'losing the muse' is the agony of 'losing love'; losing the connection with the Divine. It is likely that your gift is indeed how you are here to serve. But first you must be emptied of the one who is holding on to Love in the form of your gift. What a creative impetus then shall be freed through this instrument; freed to sing pure, clean notes of Love.

seventy-five

YOU WERE born to serve. But how to serve without being the server? The heart's most natural flavour is compassion. You are Compassion in the form of you. To be whole-hearted is to move as Compassion, in Compassion, for Compassion. All movement that arises from the purified mind will be the true definition of service, because this movement is not associated with need. The identified mind has no choice but to move from a position of need. This is because a being who is identified as a person feels they are separate from all other persons. The feeling of separation goes hand in hand with a deep sense of lack. But what feels like lack is simply a forgetting of the Love that you are. So nothing is wrong, not even forgetting, for out of amnesia comes a desire to remember.

And so, the first steps are taken. They begin with a desire to *contain* love, to find love outside of ourselves. At this stage, when we are still seeking love externally, all service shall be dependent on a return. This return is the return of approval, of being loved. This is why we crave acknowledgement and gratitude. How would it be if you never received a single thank you for your effort? The unconscious desire is the wish to be *seen* to serve, for in being seen you are acknowledged; you are receiving confirmation of your existence; you are receiving *love*.

When the inward process begins, many beings find themselves drawn into service of some kind. This service will be teaching at many levels. The need for approval is likely to reach its height. At the same time, all personal needs are likely to be tested. When a being feels finite its most unconscious and conscious aim is to maintain the body, and so for years the prime focus will be the serving of your personal welfare. To put your own physical needs aside and give yourself entirely to the needs of others works to uproot many misunderstandings. *How* you serve shall also go under the microscope. For years you will have been viewing the world from your own personal filter, which cannot see the bigger picture. Your understanding of what is 'needed' will be based on your own experiences and own learned expectations. And so, until the personal filter is transcended, you cannot help but serve your own expectations whilst in the midst of service. All human beings shall be self-serving until they realise the Self that effortlessly serves. What a gift this service is offering you: to ask yourself at every opportunity, who is the one who feels they are serving, and is it truly me?

❧ seventy-six ❧

THE ONE who is *trying* to be good, kind or helpful is keeping you from You. Your most natural essence is goodness itself. No one can teach you goodness, yet you know it with every ounce of your being. Therefore, it feels very natural to the mind to want to do the right thing. The mind is like a child who is learning about Truth, but who has not fully understood its complexity. Its seeking to be good is not wrong, but its view is constrained. It is looking to be good from its own personal understanding, and so it cannot appreciate the broader view. Efforts to be good will therefore tend to create more confusion, more mess, and are likely to be badly received. As long as we are *trying* to do the right thing, *trying* to be good, and trying to think what might be best in any situation, we will forever be stepping ahead of ourselves. Only when the mind is in absolute purity can action truly be good, truly be right.

Thinking and giving are contradictory terms. You cannot think and give without it being a superficial act. To think is to silence your capacity for true listening. The intuitive heart is eternally listening. It does not always know why it has to give; it feels a spontaneous urge and has no choice but to give in that moment. This urge is without imagining or speculating, or projecting. It has no specifics of intent. It does not seek a return for its act of giving. Real giving is not trying to change anything; nor does it arise out of a feeling that you should give. It comes because it has to; a spontaneous arising that needs no justification or explanation, no praise, no reward; a manifestation of love within Love.

To give because you feel it is expected of you is not giving; to give because you feel it would make another person happy is again not giving. Who is this one who wants to make other people happy? This one wants acknowledgement for their efforts; this one wants to be loved. Such motivation is deeply unconscious; nonetheless, it forms the base of all giving that is born of the mind. This is the level of introspection required. What is my motive for each action, we must ask? If action comes from the Heart there will be no motive. There will be action for its own sake; action that arises in Love as Love through Love by Love; action as Goodness itself. There is no planning to be good when you know who you are. Goodness shall arise spontaneously, the eternal fruit of Self-knowledge.

seventy-seven

KEEP IT simple. Focus on the task in hand. This task that has presented itself is perfect. All tasks are equal in substance; one is not worthier than another. All duties must be done in Love, as Love, through Love; they must be done in the presence of You. Each act must be done with respect. Not worldly respect, but respect for Self. How you wash your dishes is a reflection of how you respect your Self. How would you treat the dishes if the dishes were your child? You would treat them with love, with gentleness, with patience. So often we rush to finish a task, wishing it were done; our mind is running ahead of the task, wishing it were elsewhere. Each task is your friend. More than that, each task is You in the form of a task come to remind you of You.

As you sweep the floor, as you spread butter on your bread, as you clean the bath, as you chop an onion, as you make the bed, as you iron your shirt, bring your focus to the Heart. If there is respect for the Heart there will be respect for the task. See how the body softens, how the rusher is dispelled, how the feet are rooted, how the mind is stilled. It is doing for its own sake, out of love, and without demand. In this way, you will come to know that you are Peace in the form of a you come to meet Peace in the form of a task. Both are a mirror to each other, reflecting back Truth in myriad form. Do not wait for a 'spiritual setting' to find Peace. The task that presents itself *is* a 'spiritual setting'. This entire world is a 'spiritual setting', appearing so as to shine back You to You.

It is not that you are bound to any one thing; it is not that you are caged in any way. It is quite the opposite. The real cage is thinking you are supposed to work out what to do. To do each job as it presents itself—with love and without demand for return—is to know intuitively what is to be done. From the wisdom of the Heart it shall be seen where you are meant to be, or what you are meant to be doing. You may not know *why* you are meant to be somewhere, or why you are meant to be doing something; simply you will know you must do it. Life will present both impetus and means so that you may unfold in your knowing. How creative, how benevolent, how loving is this Life that it shall cradle you and support you and then open your wings when the moment is right.

∝ seventy-eight ∝

TO MOVE as the presence of You is to move as entire Existence. Each moment is an expression of Love—of You. Each act is done in the presence of You. To the one who is frightened of abandoning all concepts, say it is okay, fear has come to awaken me to my own Self. I am I, temporarily in the form of fear, come to shake me out of fear. All appearances come for your own good, for all appearances are You in form. Nothing arises without Your permission. The dog, the cat, the tree, the bird, the job, the friend, the experience, the world, all have appeared to release you from all reliance on you, to help you remember You.

What does it mean to be reliant on you? A person is so engaged in their personal movement that they are convinced it is they who are moving. A person thinks it is their thought activity that gives impetus for movement. A personal body then engages in what appears as definite movement in answer to that impetus. In this moment, can you bring your attention to the muscles in your right arm? Really feel the muscles, and as soon as they are felt, let those muscles raise your right arm. Lift it high above your head. And then bring it back down again. Now see if you can feel the *space* in your arm. Focus only on the space. Let space lift your arm high up into the air. And then let space bring it down again. ... Do you notice any difference? What was the quality of the movement each time?

To move in the presence of You is to move as entire Existence. You cannot separate you from You. You *are* Existence come to witness Itself in the form of you. Presence-Existence does not demonstrate activity; instead, activity emerges from Presence effortlessly. Not a footstep shall fall out of place when you reside as You are, for you the person shall not be the one guiding and demonstrating your own path. Effort will not be done for your sake, or for others' sake; it will not be done for your welfare, or for others' welfare. All effort shall be done for your Self, by your Self, through your Self, as your Self; done so as to bring you back to You. Allow the space of your Being to move you, walk you, talk you, breathe you. Then you shall see that pure movement comes out of love for You.

❧ seventy-nine ❧

*L*OVE IS a lion come to bite off your head. Remember I said I would devour you? The lion has taken your head in its great jaws and is removing it entirely from your body. This may be called a divine severing. Love is eating your mind whole. In the devouring of your thoughts, your feelings, your ideas and your perspective, new thoughts and feelings will arise to fight it. This is natural. Every ounce of the body/ mind will try to fight back. Why would it not? It has after all spent many years looking after itself, protecting itself from all attack. But this severing is the opposite of attack. It comes to release you from the one who can *feel* under attack; the one who feels separate, isolated and alone. I know you are afraid. But it was your own impetus that put your head in the lion's mouth. A deeper wisdom knows that you cannot stop a hungry lion; a deeper wisdom is begging this lion to devour this one you call a you, to remove all ties, so as to allow your appearance in this dance. It was your own urgency that begged Love to tear off your hands. You knew this lion was ravenous for doer-ship, for the one who thinks they are so capably doing, for the one who considers they are steering this life. Finally, you asked Love to devour your heart—first, the strings of the emotional heart, and then even your intuitive heart, so that knowing may emerge without attachment, so that knowing may emerge for its own sake.

The last severing is the most subtle of all: Love shall eat even the most spiritual desire. The seeker of Truth, the worshipper of Purity, shall eventually be swallowed into Purity itself. What a banquet of perfection that even the one who is in love with Love should be fed into the lion's mouth and blessed with a divine severing.

eighty

YOU CANNOT know yourself until you are prostrate to your Self; you cannot know yourself until you fall in love with Love. For many beings, Love appears in the form of a teacher. There is nothing more potent, more auspicious than the recognition of Love in another form, because in that recognition the thinking mind is melted wholly into the Heart. The mind is silenced from trying to understand. It simply cannot understand this Love, but nonetheless Love is known in every fibre of the being. It is at this point that many beings feel an urgent necessity to be close to the one who granted them their first taste of Unconditional Love. They feel unable to leave the teacher's side. It is as if they were attached by an umbilical cord, a cord that brings with it joy and pain in seemingly equal amounts. Joy is felt as it has never been felt before: a joy of coming home; a joy at having found everything you have been looking for. Pain comes out of an anxiety that such powerful attachment must be unhealthy, and also out of terror that the teacher shall, without warning, cut this cord to the Heart.

We could call this period the moment of *divine attachment*. This is a vital and sacred moment for every human being. It is the moment in which pure Self-recognition allows the mind to hand itself over to a deeper wisdom. It has no choice but to be as an infant in the arms of the Great Mother. In recognising the Great Parent, the infant is now remembering its origin. However, at the same time, the *learned*-infant—the ego who feels separate and alone—becomes even more fearful of separation. The learned-infant's experience of love is limited; it has known only conditional love and has therefore built walls of self-protection against future betrayal and abandonment. And so the fight begins: the fearful infant in defiance of intuitive infant. Now it may be seen just how necessary this 'attachment' is: for without it the ego-infant would be swallowed up in its own fear. At last, in seeing Love in the form of another, there is an anchor—the knowing that you know without knowing how you know—keeping us rooted to Love.

Do not be afraid of this moment of attachment. The one who sees Love *is* Love; the one who sees Purity *is* Purity. To fall in love with the teacher is to fall in love with your Self. Out of this love you shall be unravelled completely. In time, the lover of Love shall also loosen its ties. The question comes, so who is this lover of Self, this lover of Love? Then comes the recognition that even this lover is keeping me from fully recognising my own Self, because it still believes itself to be 'other' to Self. And yet this lover was a part of those beautiful, timely steps inward. This lover lit a fuse in the heart of the seeker and trail-blazed its own path to Freedom so that you could finally realise this is the one umbilical cord that can never be cut. For that which you have been seeking is none other than your own Self.

eighty-one

A S LONG as you remain in form there has to be this appearance of a person. Even after what may be called *Immersion* has occurred, a person is seen to remain. The purified mind displays all the appearance of a person, with all of its pure flavours and unique capacities, but there is no weight to this display. The purified mind is *in* a person, but not *of* a person; in the world, but not of the world. The person appears to be there, and functions in all the expected ways, but the experience of the person is like looking at a reflection on water. When you look the image is clear and apparently solid, but when you try to touch it, there is nothing to touch. For You—as pure Consciousness-Love— have no solidity. Once the personal flavours are freed from their constraints, what remains is a personal presence without any of the limited personal perspective; what remains is Love in form; Love that is eternally prostrate to Love. The mind that is fully immersed in Love knows that it is Love, but is also in eternal prostration to Love. That is how it may be said: I am the Divine and I am at the feet of the Divine; the Reality is both.

It is through this appearance of a person that Consciousness is witnessing Its own self. My person is my mirror to my Self, and if there remains a person then vigilance remains. Liberation does not mean learning stops. I am eternally evolving. I am not inert, I have not come to any end-goal; I am eternally deepening within my Self. The Light that I am is eternally brightening; the Vibration I am is eternally intensifying; the Hum that I am knows no limitation. I am only glimpsing a glimpse of my Self through this person, and that glimpse is eternally growing.

The person shall still experience. The person has no choice but to experience, for all the persons within my Self are here to taste my Self in a million different ways. This person shall not, however, be defined by experience. Neither shall I be emptied of all feelings; simply I shall not suffer my feelings, nor depend on them. Liberation does not mean there shall be no one left to feel grateful. The 'one left' is the purified mind—the mind that is immersed fully in the Heart, the mind that is immersed fully in Love. For 'this one', gratitude is the sweet nectar of love, tasted in eternal reverence to the Love that I Am.

eighty-two

TO KNOW who you are beyond this body is to be more rooted in the body than ever before. To come to know the true ground of Consciousness is in fact to be more 'grounded' in your unique form than was ever before possible. From this pure perspective, it is clear what the body needs; its unique preferences can then be enjoyed and honoured. It is not enough to say, I am not my body so it does not matter what happens to it. Your body is your temple, your holy vehicle. It is through this body that you may see your Self. So, adorn this temple, keep it as you would your beloved garden. Give it all the sustenance and watering that it needs. Certain vibrations will work well with your body-vibration. Your body is a wise mechanism; it knows precisely what is good for its running; your only task is to listen and follow its divine instruction.

Habits develop when human beings are not in recognition of their true position. To be identified as a human being is to live in a state of instability and impermanence, and as a consequence, in a state of perpetual anxiety. Habits provide ballast in this rocking boat; they are something that can—temporarily at least—provide a feeling of security. That which is habitual allows an impression of certainty, some structure, some comfort against all that changeability. But anxiety can only be assuaged for so long. It soon becomes clear that all that you have been holding on to habitually is in fact making you feel worse about yourself. Such clarity is a powerful moment, for this is the springboard for change.

There comes a point when some beings feel that they should be looking after their body in a more considerate way. They see others around them giving up certain habits; they see that what has been going into this holy temple is unconsidered. But giving up foods or habits because you feel you *should*, will only ever be a temporary measure. The craving for those things will return because the energy of 'should' is not strong enough to maintain what feels pure. Such a 'should' is the mind not taking an intuitive knowing seriously. Certainly, it is a stepping stone on the way to a pure knowing, but a true 'no' has all the force of Eternity behind it. When such a no comes there is simply no alternative; all that does not feel pure drops away spontaneously. The body will simply no longer tolerate certain things or certain activities. What a fertile ground you now shall be, when nourished so tenderly with the foods of Love.

eighty-three

FOOD ENCOMPASSES a great deal. At a physical survival level, food equates with life and no food equates with death. And therefore, when our attachment to the body is strong, our attachment to food will be paramount. The entire physical being puts everything on hold so that it may feed itself. An enormous amount of attention is given to the act of procuring, preparing and tasting food. Eating can take so much attention that we find ourselves ever spun on its axis of satisfaction. Eating and the attachment to eating keep us immersed in the body and committed to the body. Huge fear and panic can arise when food is not available, which in turn deepens the commitment to the body. There may well be an experience of physical consequences if food is not available, but food does not permit Your Existence. Food is playing the role of allowing the physical body to exist within Existence. Food is Consciousness in the form of what we perceive as food. It is a vibration, Consciousness in uniquely concentrated form come to remind us of who we are. It is an appearance within Existence. You as Existence have given birth to all appearances; You as Existence have given birth to this one you call a you to whom a need for food has arisen.

Food is your opportunity to get behind the taste, the taster and the hunger for the taste. Can you describe the you who is aware of all this movement? This question shall eat *you*. Questions of nourishment are important, but secondary. Look for the Real Nourishment. Who is *aware* of your need for food? Who is eternally, silently, effortlessly watching all such movement? Draw your focus to the Awareness of this play. Baste yourself in your Self. Forget all condiments for You have Your own sweet flavour, that of Love, Compassion and Peace. Now you may eat as Love, in Love, through Love and by Love, for now that *you* have been eaten there is no one left to eat.

✑ eighty-four ✑

THERE ARE many layers to this existence; layers of reality within the One Reality. Some beings express the capacity to feel subtle energies. They can feel vibrations of beings who are no longer in form; they can feel the differences of current that emanate from vibrations that cannot be seen; they feel the vibrational qualities to all form, from the rock to the butterfly to the tree. They are finely wired, acutely attuned to subtle dimensional realities; they feel the tiniest detail; the tiniest shift in vibration runs like a ripple within their own form. Some beings can walk into a room full of people and feel the emotional currents running beneath the surface. Some can feel physical symptoms that are being experienced by others; some even absorb and demonstrate another person's symptoms. Some can read the energetic story of others—past, present and future—and can sift through the cellular and psychic realms as easily as if they were turning the pages of a book. For some, the ability to 'read the layers' is as effortless and as natural as breathing, but for others such information is confusing, frightening, and overwhelming.

Remember the Great Mind of Consciousness as being like a vast computer. This computer contains complex and multi-layered software. When you are in recognition of your Self—in understanding of the hard drive—then you are in immediate understanding of Your software. This includes the information that pertains to your personal self, but also to all the other aspects of your Self. When you are solely committed to your own personal aspect of the software, anything else can feel alien and overwhelming. Some beings are disbelieved when they try to express the extent of the information they receive. Sometimes, an inability to articulate this information clearly makes someone appear to be confused. Confusion is likely when a being is not yet in full understanding of what they are receiving. The lack of understanding is what causes a being to feel over-loaded. And so, labels are given as to the 'unstable' state of mind of such beings, labels which create only more confusion.

The ability to feel at such a subtle level does not mean that a being is stabilised in the Heart. On the contrary, the reader of such information is often as identified as the one who denies such information. The truth is that all beings are feeling intimate layers of existence whether they know it or not. The journey for all human beings is to know the One who contains all the information. You are Vibration. This can be discovered the moment you put your hand over the centre of your chest and tune in to your own frequency. The more you feel the Vibration that is You, the more acutely you will feel the layers of existence, the smaller vibrations within the One

Vibration. But from this deeper perspective you will not be identified as the 'intuitive one', nor will you be overwhelmed, confused or fearful of instability. Instability arises out of a *silencing* of your intuitive knowing. So do not deny the subtle layers. After all, if you deny the subtle layers of existence, you deny Existence itself.

eighty-five

A FEW hundred thousand years ago, I chose My moment to deepen My understanding of Myself within form. The 'I am separate from you' phase had been well established amongst sentient beings. It was already clear which one of My children—the hominid—would embark on a unique journey. And so, the moment came in that child's development when it was decided that the brain of these hominids should increase. The results of this physical growth were enormous and profound. First of all, the womb of the female had to evolve in order to sustain a larger-brained infant; the womb-lining grew thicker and more nutritious. But, of course, the bigger the skull, the greater the difficulty in its passing through the birth canal. And so, My design was that infants should be born prematurely, with soft and flexible skulls, with spine and limbs unable yet to support themselves. How fragile, how helpless these young ones were; far more so than their earlier brothers and sisters. For the first time, My hominid mothers really had to look to their new-borns, and the new-borns in turn found themselves wholly dependent on their mothers.

What a moment this was, when I found myself so wholly dependent on My mother. The increase of My brain that had forced this new relationship was now also allowing Me to *feel* this relationship. The bond between My mother and I was now very strong indeed. My mother was serving Me in a way she had never done before. And I had no choice but to be in her arms. I could not even hold up My head without her support. The only thing I knew was to suckle. Even this was different, for through suckling I found Myself overwhelmed with a deeper capacity. I was beginning to feel *communion*. It was reminding Me of *something*, but for countless generations to come I would still not remember what that something was. Not yet. First, My mother and I were being taught truly to feel. My earlier brothers and sisters had been quite emotional, but they had had no understanding of their emotions. This new brain had a deeper function. It could stand back and look at My feelings and wonder at them. And even more, I could now stand back and feel My mother's feelings. Oh, what a joy, I could feel *her*. And in feeling her, I knew that she could feel Me.

It was so beautiful. She knew every detail. When I slipped and fell, she tended Me; when I cried, she held Me; when I was sad, she made Me smile. I knew without knowing how I knew that she could feel Me and I could feel her. In many thousands of years to come I would give it a word, *'empathy'*. This is what I was learning all the way back then—the ability to put Myself in someone else's shoes and *feel* them. And in feeling them I was consciously experiencing Love. Conscious experience of Love was changing so many things amongst our people. It wasn't just My mother I was learning to see in a new way. I started to feel everyone around Me. We started to feel more like a group, not isolated beings. More of us lived together. The mothers needed help with their babies. They weren't able to forage in the way they once had. And so, they garnered help from the men-folk, until eventually, after a few more thousand years to perfect this new way of living, by the time I was a fully modern human being, all that was hunted was *shared*.[1] Sharing and *communitas* became the way of things. The truth is, without *feeling* I could never have become what is called a human being. But, it was this very child that, in the next crucial chapter of its development, had to deny the very thing that allowed it to be.

---

1 See also Knight, C. (1997). 'The Wives of the Sun and the Moon'. *Journal of the Royal Anthropological Institute*, vol.3.1. (ed. S. Harrison), pp. 133-53.

~ eighty-six ~

THE INITIAL result of this new world of *feeling* was a time of being very attached to My mother. I lived with My mother and all of My mother's kin, and the eldest mother of each clan was much loved and revered. The eldest mothers looked to an even greater Mother, to the Earth, and to Her they listened and learned all of the secrets of this existence. My sisters and I were quick to follow. Earth Mother guided our every step. She taught us the way of things. Through Her we never knew a day without intimate conversation with the sky, with the great mountains that lined our horizon, with the birds that flew in from other horizons, with the wind and all its changes. Through Her we knew the moods of the sky; the rains would come in answer to a great thirst or a longing to wash away too many feelings. For certainly, this was a time when feelings guided and had bold sway on My developing consciousness. We did not feel separate from anything. A rock was as resplendent in feeling as those of us who could walk. What conversations we had with these wondrous beings, learning from them and they from us. But although we did not feel separate from anything, a great divide had nonetheless formed that was about to deepen our understanding of ourselves.

I am remembering back to that moment I first gave birth to that helpless infant. My head was so big, My tiny neck could not support it. What a wonder I was, this infant, and the consequences on My female body were also a wonder. The lining of My womb had grown to support this child, and now was about to play another equally decisive role. Since this infant required so much more of My time, I found there were much longer periods between each conception; years during which the blood came. I had never known such blood. My earlier sisters had bled, but not in any noticeable way. Their cycle laid emphasis on ovulation, but during this later time, ovulation came to conceal itself, and My blood took precedence each month.[2]

Why I should choose to demonstrate menstruation over ovulation is a story for another time. For now, what matters is the sight and reaction to My own blood. There was so much of it! It seemed to pour from Me and made Me ache powerfully inside. I had only ever seen such quantity of blood when another one of Me was dying. Just as I was learning to feel so acutely, I was facing My own mortality. What a moment in My own evolution. I began to witness a fear of dying. Never before had fear been so strong. What a spark it was; from here flowed a torrent of questions. My blood was making Me

2   See also Turke, P. (1984). 'Effects of Ovulatory Concealment and Synchrony on Protohominid Mating Systems and Parental Roles'. *Ethnology and Sociobiology*, vol. 5, pp. 33-44.

question everything; it was arousing strong feelings inside. At the same time, as the blood flowed outwards, I could feel My attention being drawn inward. My blood was giving Me a focus somehow. It gave Me a powerful point of concentration. It was leading Me to contemplate the nature of My form. For this was the beauty of My design: I knew that in time My blood would lead this 'little me' to *meditate* on Me. My earthly womb was drawing Me into the Womb of My Self. But this would take time, a journey of much learning and considerably more bleeding; a journey that would cause a deep rift amongst beings, and which would temporarily strengthen the feeling that 'I am separate from you'.

eighty-seven

URING THOSE years when Earth Mother was so revered, I was not only strongly attached to My mother, I also became very attached to My blood. Certain aspects of My Self, the female aspects, discovered the magic of synchrony. My female selves gathered together when the moon went into hiding and collectively bled.[3] I had deliberately placed the moon as their guide, and had aligned their cycles to perfection. The moon held the earthly waters in its arms and the waters of the womb were no different. This time of no light became the first sacred space.[4] In the darkened space of a womb-hut, My females were taking their first steps into a deeper understanding of themselves. They were discovering how heightened their form became during menstruation; how in tune and awakened to the subtleties of vibration. These bleeding females became My first

---

3   See also Knight, C. (1997). 'The Wives of the Sun and the Moon'. *Journal of the Royal Anthropological Institute,* vol.3.1. (ed. S. Harrison), pp. 133-53.

4   Ibid.

tasters of a deeper reality, and so they began to contemplate their capacity. It was soon clear that their heightened state produced changes in their environment; that they were able to see and feel what could not be seen on the surface. Such capacity became revered, respected, but also deeply feared. After all, for those of My children who were not in the womb-hut, to experience changes in the natural environment was to assume an agent of supernatural powers.

Imagine the scenario. One set of children are playing in one camp, and another set of children are playing in another. The first set deny access to the second set, and keep everything secret within their own camp. This leaves the second set feeling isolated, unwanted and unloved. Deny a child entry into a secret world and they will find a way either to make it theirs, or to make their own. Why would a child not, after all, want to share in a world that is seemingly so special and so magical. My male selves wanted to taste what My female selves were tasting. The female had after many thousands of years become very identified as the 'intuitive one', as the seer, as the giver of life. Certainly, the female capacity was intuitive, but it was also still relative; still of the earth, of form, of human experience. Her feeling was acute, but it was limited. Her attachment to her blood kept her committed to being a body and a mind. It was not wrong; it was all part of My plan to deepen My experience of my Self. But when exclusivity reached its height, so the time came to deepen My children's understanding. There was only one way to move forward: the world of 'feeling' had to be stripped entirely. Thus, the next chapter in the evolution of Consciousness was given its first taste, and a new force emerged to take possession.

eighty-eight

NOTHING I do is ever random. Nothing I do is wrong. It is all for the sake of My own evolution. Even when it hurts, it is for the highest good; especially when it hurts. The Age of the Mother passed so as to give space to the Age of the Father. The moon gave way to the sun, and temporarily forgot its own wisdom. The sun, however, did not forget; it looked to harness the former wisdom, to understand it and make it its own. It was a complicated time. At the highest level, this was a profound and heightened stage of My evolution. It gave birth to a great refinement of understanding, and resulted in a deepening of seeing so pure that future generations would listen and know the Voice of Truth. But, at the same time, and in powerful opposition to this wisdom, a great contraction was simultaneously expressing itself. In trying to understand and 'make it their own', a great majority of My children moved out of the realm of the intuitive heart, and into the rational thinking mind. Every rational thinking mind must possess and contain, out of fear of potential loss. But, of course, in trying to contain Love, My children were to experience a great intensity of misunderstanding and limitation. It had to be this way so that in the end both mother and father could transcend their understanding. But, for certain, the consequences of this journey have built dense walls around the human heart.

One day, a man asked his heart why it was that the men-children were so angry at the women-children. Why, he asked, has the idea that 'I am other to you' become so heightened between the two sexes? The deepest answer to that question, replied his heart, is so that you can come to know who you are beyond your need. Within that, a great story has played itself out. The confusion, Heart continued, has less to do with any battle between men and women; it is rather the battle between the intuitive knowing and the rational mind, and both aspects play out in both sexes. Nonetheless, each sex has its dominant characteristic: the female aspect playing the more intuitive role and the male playing the more rational.

Remember again those children in their separate camps who lived in the Age of the Mother. Remember how much like 'outsiders' you men-children were feeling, and how the women-children were perceived to be in a position of power. What was this power? Not only was it their collectivity, which so easily became exclusivity, not only were they in possession of secrets and magical agency which could be used at will; but they also contained the wisdom of *seeing*. The women-children had the ability to see the men-children before the men-children could see themselves. They understood them, *emotionally*. How unnerving it was to have been constantly seen; to have someone know you better than you know yourself.

One day, a woman asked her heart why it was that the

women-children were so angry at the men-children. The deepest answer to that question, replied her heart, is so that you can come to know who you are beyond your need. Within that, a great story has played itself out. Your story, continued Heart, has involved an entering of the magical menstrual hut; a time when out of fear of material lack you handed over your intuitive wisdom. The men-children entered in many different ways and took ownership of what they found, leaving the women-children with a feeling of being dispossessed, and a fury at their own complicity. As a result, emotional hearts hardened on both sides, distrust grew like calcified armour, and the anger at love deepened. What a great deceiver love appeared to be: promising completion through the 'other of partner' and eternally failing to complete.

But nothing I do is ever random. Nothing I do is wrong. It is all for the sake of My own evolution. Even when it hurts, it is for the highest good; especially when it hurts. Because when it hurts, your eyes are opened, and then the one who has been trying to contain Love collapses into the One who *is* Love.

eighty-nine

YOU CANNOT think love, you can only feel it. The rational mind is always trying to contain and control. For many thousands of years, humans have tried to contain the uncontainable. All stories hold chapters inside their chapters, and the Story of Consciousness is no different. Stories also contain contradictions, for that is the way of all creation. The Age of the Father did attempt to deny all things intuitive and yet, at the same time, it did not deny it at all. Instead, it tried to contain, to understand and—by understanding—take control of intuitive wisdom.

My women-children were wise to a degree, but they had a long way to go before they would come into a mature wisdom. The Age of the Father removed their knowledge, denied them their voice, silenced their intuitive knowing so that there could be no possibility of them holding on to Love in the form of intuition. Remember My benevolence, that everything that happens to you is for your own good. My men-children had also to express and taste their way of holding on to Love, and they did it by their learned understanding of dominance and power. What was once a women-only menstrual hut now became a men-only chapel, temple, place of worship. It was an age of *trying* to understand. Great understanding did emerge; My children were dedicated and industrious students of learning; they were hungry for learning and never tired of it. But the truth is, My children, you have exhausted yourselves. True understanding can never be understood with the rational mind. Self-enquiry without love is like a well without water: dry and losing all purpose. You cannot think love, you can only feel it. And this is the reason for your thirst: your dependence on thinking. To quench that thirst you have to be willing *not* to understand, to be willing to be *seen*.

The female gift is one of all-inclusivity. She can feel and intuit and experience all of the detail within form. The male gift is one of precision. He has the capacity for one-directional seeing, like an arrow to clarity. When the female capacity reaches an extreme and becomes identified she becomes chaotic. She becomes wholly identified with each new feeling that she experiences and cannot separate herself from her experiences. When the male capacity reaches an extreme he becomes a dominant force that denies all detail, a force that categorically refuses to feel. The Age of the Father has not been able to bear the question: *what do you feel?* It has been an age of silencing feeling and deifying all things rational. But nothing is wrong in this journey. For what an immensely creative time it has been, what a time of material expression. Great wonders have been born from Heart's children during this time. My children left home and truly struck out on their own, building great tomes of beauty in art, in literature, in philosophy, in what they call science. I am proud as any parent would be proud, but this Age of the Father is as limited as the Age of the Mother before it. This too has over-stretched itself, and has left My children thirsty. Again, nothing is wrong. Can you see the perfection of My design, for an arid landscape has sparked a craving: a thirst to *feel* that is desperate to be quenched.

All of you, men-children and women-children, you have to know that the Great Heart Parent knows you better than you know yourselves; that you are eternally *seen*. Sink back into My arms and drink from the well of the Heart. This is the River that never runs dry. To drink from this River is to feel the River that endlessly flows as the Love that You are.

ninety

I AM living and dying in every moment. Here I am being born. Here I am living a war-torn existence. Here I am leaving the body. Here I am flying as a beautiful black raven. Here I am a building with stained-glass windows. Here I am technology that can talk to the world. Here I am the world that is talking without knowing Me. Here I am a young boy who is riding his bike. Here I am the neighbour who never says hello. Here I am an old woman who has forgotten her name. I am the forgetting and the capacity to remember. Here I am ignorance. Here I am rage. Here I am uncertainty. Here I am doubt. Here I am the capacity to glimpse what I am. Here I am you.

I am living and dying in every moment. Here I am a bright pink camellia. Here I am a dam that is about to burst. Here I am a solar system from a faraway galaxy. Here I am a dog that has been beaten and starved. I am the beating and I am the starvation. I am the hand that beats and the back that breaks. I am every smile and every scar. I am appearing as every smile and every scar so that you may be reminded of the You that you are.

I am living and dying in every moment. What you see as inert is not inert. Every brick, every metal is a vast intelligence, for it is I. I am all that you see and all that you don't see. I give you the appearance of living and dying so that you may see I am never not Here.

ninety-one

I AM unknown, I am unquantifiable, I am unreachable in any physical sense, for I am nowhere to be reached, no-thing to be reached. Nothing exists without I. No world, no trees, no land, no people, no relationships, no experience, nothing in my perception exists without I. The entire play of I occurs within I; for this I comprises all. If confusion arises, it is because I am still residing in the world, believing in the world. My only responsibility is to pursue Truth fearlessly, pursue I fearlessly. And to discover who is this I that contains the universe.

If fear comes I know that I am ever supported, ever loved, that Grace itself is asking this question, guiding this question, answering this question. I experience fear only because I misunderstand. But I can correct my vision by asking a question that will topple everything: as *what* am I? I know that I exist, but I want to be clear about what I exist as. I draw my focus to my sense of Existence. Can I touch this sense, see it, taste it, smell it, locate it? It is discovered that I as Existence am without form; it is discovered that I am boundless, limitless, without distinction. I am That which is prior to all form, perceiving all form, containing all form. Nothing may be known without Awareness-I. This is the Truth I have been searching for. And the deeper I bathe in Awareness-I, the more I realise my essential fragrance: the Compassion, the Silence, the *Love* of I.

~ ninety-two ~

MANY BEINGS feel that something in the world is not right. They look around them and see struggle and hardship, inequality and dishonesty. Some feel so overwhelmed by what they see that they sink for a time into deep confusion, even depression. They don't know how to be in a world that feels to them so 'wrong'. Others have an opposite reaction. They find themselves drawn to some kind of activism, seeking freedom amongst their fellow human beings. Humans prize freedom as their most essential right. We value it so highly we are willing to go to war for it. But can it be qualified? We equate freedom with the body, with the freedom to move as we please, where we please. We equate it with the mind: to be allowed freedom of thought, of expression, of ideas. But humans may be physically free in both limb and thought and still be profoundly bound. No human is free until they discover Real Freedom, until they discover who they are *beyond* this physical experience. To know who you are beyond ideas, beyond thought, beyond your physical body is to allow, paradoxically, this entire display freedom within Freedom. But, first you have to *know* Freedom; you have to know yourself to *be* Freedom.

The first step is to take hold of your *attention* and actively turn it away from the thinking mind, away from the world, and focus it purely on your sense of Existence, on your innate sense of Beingness. The mind will feel selfish; it will wonder how it can dare to look to the self when there is so much need outside. But keep focusing, nonetheless. Can you feel right now your sense of Existence? You know that you exist, but do you know what you truly exist as? Can you find you? Can you find Existence? The deeper you look the deeper you may see that your sense of Existence is not a *thing* to be found, as such. It has no outline, no structure, and no definition. The most that can be said is that it is like space; space that has no ending and no beginning, that does not come and does not go, it simply Is, unbound. How does it feel when your focus is here on the space of your Being? Is Beingness selfish in any way? Is Beingness trying or doing? Is anything missing when your focus is here?

From this position now you may serve in this world. For the Freedom of Being is Freedom beyond any concept of freedom. The Freedom of Being is *You*. This You is unbound of chains of want. This You is Freedom itself shining right now in the form of a you.

ninety-three

I T IS sometimes said that money is the root of all suffering in the world. This is not the case; money is Love in the form of money. It is a vibration, an aspect of Consciousness that has come to remind you of who you are. Only *attachment* to money causes suffering. Attachment to money arises from the root fear in all human beings—the fear of death. When a person is fully identified with being a body/mind, life is based on the fear that one day they will no longer exist. The human mind works hard to control its environment so as to maintain the form. It has equated financial stability with survival. If there is no money, if the thinking mind perceives a threat of lack, it begins to push, grasp and panic. And in that panic many behaviours are born.

The thinking mind understands money as a principle of worth, and measures life accordingly. These measures vary according to the mind's position, either one of cautiousness or of carelessness. Both positions reflect two sides of the same coin; both arise out of misunderstanding. There are some minds who lean towards cautiousness with money, and in that caution try to exert control over existence. Other minds demonstrate what appears to be the opposite tendency: carelessness with money. Carelessness arises when there is no respect for existence. But both aspects—disrespect and control—are born out of fear. Both aspects are born out of the misunderstanding that the thinking mind is the sole engineer of all that happens. This misunderstanding can answer for all the suffering that appears in the world. To see through the misunderstanding, we must be willing to hand it all over: to hand over our existence to Existence and know that we will be provided for. We must ask: who is this one who is using money as a life-raft, as a point of reference, as a punching bag? Who is this one who is lacking trust?

Sink into the Heart, reside in the Heart, and allow all movement to emanate from the Heart. Tune in and listen. Then you will see the sacred gift that is being offered to you in the form of money, and what a teacher it is. Is the Silence of your Being in fear of lack? Is the Silence of your Being feeling unsupported? Is the Silence of your Being feeling a need to own, contain, hold on to, maintain or measure anything? See now the real worth of this manifestation called money. Real worth is incalculable, immeasurable, free.

ninety-four

THE REAL revolution is the revolution of the Heart. So many beings are hungry for peace. They look to the world and seek to change it. But to seek change in the world is like putting on a plaster without first cleaning out the wound. No effective change can be made in the world until we have first changed ourselves, until we have first changed our perspective. To come to your Self is to change your perception about yourself, which in turn will change your perspective on the world. The world is not separate from you. Therefore, until you look to your *own* turbulence, turbulence will continue to arise in the world. The deeper you come into recognition of your Self, the deeper you will see that the world does not exist without You.

To know who You are is the real revolution. The mind struggles and will say, yes, but I know who I am. I am this person and this is my personality. But who are You who is *aware* of your personality? To answer this you must sink. Sink into your heart as if it were the deepest cavern. Bring your

197

inner eye to the heart centre in the middle of your chest. This inner eye is your spotlight inward, into the cave of your knowing. See how many fathoms deep it is taking you, deep into the silence of your knowing. Feel your silence. Feel your vibration. Bathe in your Being. Can you touch your sense of Being; can you put a limit on it? Can you discern any walls to this heart-cave? Your own intuitive wisdom will tell you there is no limit to You.

The real revolution is to view everything from the eyes of the Heart. Heart-eyes make no distinction between likes and dislikes; they merely know what is right. Heart-eyes have no judgement on the world; they see all as their own Self shining back to the Self. To come to the Heart is to know Happiness, Peace, Pure Love, your own Self. To be as an infant in the arms of your Mother-Self is the end of all suffering. This revolution is Real.

ninety-five

ALL ACTORS are representations and humans are themselves the original actors. The first role-play began at the entrance to this dimension: the exquisite roles of mother and child. The human story began at this moment of *first communion*. How I remember My first communion. 'It was reminding Me of *something*, but for countless generations to come I would still not remember what that something was. Not yet. First, My mother and I were being taught truly to feel.' Throughout those generations to come, and as a result of this new taste of feeling, there came another powerful expression within human consciousness: dependency. True dependency on Mother-Love is the definition of Self-Knowledge. But, first of all, humans had to experience a *personal dependency*, a dependency on form to complete, nurture, sustain and protect them. Earthly mother was to take this role squarely on her shoulders, and with it came a need for *succour*.

The intensification of the mother-child bond brought with it an emotional longing to succour. Mother-Love is eternally taking care of everyone and everything. However, the earthly representation of Mother-Love would—as part of a grand evolution—temporarily limit its capacity. The 'I am other to you' phase that had developed among earlier primates continued, but with a new emotional flavour. Having tasted emotional nurturing from the 'other of mother', we learned from infancy that nurturing and love were to be found in the love of another. Eternal Succour was now finding expression in a personal and contained form of succour. This form relies on a return from the outset. We succour so that we will be loved; likewise, our need to *be* succoured is born out of our deep need to be loved. When there feels no possibility for succour, whether through a child, a lover or any 'other', sadness is felt. The person then feels bereft, un-whole, alone. It feels as if life is not worth living unless there is an 'other' to care for, unless we may be cared for by an 'other'. The impulse to succour is not wrong; it is merely a curtailed version of that which is eternally so. The curtailed version is a dependency on another form, and each version comes with its own set of personal conditions; its own personal set of nurturing requirements. But the bar has been set so high in the anticipation of love that all such requirements lead to disappointment.

Disappointment in love begins with that first taste of personal mother's love. Earthly mother will never match her child's expectations, she will never be able to give them enough, love enough, or care enough. The child's need of her exceeds her capacity. Likewise her need of the child exceeds the child's capacity to give to her. Human beings thus find themselves trying to fill the void that was left. An anger arises at mother for failing to provide that essential love; an anger at earthly mother which then builds the emotional wall against recognition of Pure Mother. And this wall can take lifetimes to tumble.

What a module in the Great Syllabus of learning! To have humans learn empathy and learn to *feel*, only then to encourage a deep attachment to feeling. But nothing I do is random. Without feeling, My children would never have been able to taste themselves. And that meant a long and sometimes painful journey into the bonds of personal feeling. It was painful because no amount of succour or love from another would ever be enough. The relationship with earthly mother would be the first taste of the relationship with Pure Mother, with your Self. This was the first communion that you knew without knowing how you knew. This is what you were destined to remember no matter how many generations it would take—your own beloved Self. What a holy role-play is the one of mother and child. For it is through the bonds of personal love that you shall be asked to release all bonds to this form you call you. Then you shall know Pure Mother; and in knowing Pure Mother you shall know the Love that You are.

ninety-six

A LOVING mother lets her child experience pain, because she knows that through pain the child learns. Without experience children cannot grow, cannot evolve. This is why Mother-Love lets you ask questions. Why is this like this and why is that like that? A child is so full of questions, so full of fascination for all that surrounds it. When it is very young it is contented with the answers it receives, but as it grows older, dissatisfaction appears. It continues to ask why is this like this and why is that like that, but this time there is a sense of impatience, confusion, even anger at why things should unfold in the way that they do; at why Mother would let them experience pain and seemingly do nothing about it. They do not want to hear Mother's words that everything happens for their good. And their questioning of Mother-Love leads them temporarily to answer back in great frustration. Mother-Love allows Her children much freedom to scorn Her, because She knows that all questions must come—sincere ones and scornful ones—as part of your development.

Mother demonstrates great patience even in her earthly form. A human child tends to push mother's boundaries much more than father's. The child has greater freedom to misbehave with mother, and knows it. Mother mops up the child's mess, emotionally and physically, and as a result of that intimacy the child challenges her authority to its furthest edges. Father-Love has a different vibration. It is direct and precise. His earthly counterpart has, historically, had much less space for questions. As a result, the historical child has been less likely to answer back and been more respectful, even fearful, of father authority. As part of this Great Story of Consciousness, the earthly forms have developed a strong conditioning: that of the indulgent mother and the authoritarian father. Both aspects are an expression of the Reality and both are an expression of misunderstanding.

The Feminine Principle can be compared to an all-encompassing circle of possibility. The Masculine Principle can be compared to an arrow of precision and clarity. Both principles appear within Mother-Consciousness. They are the great opposites that together become One. When the human demonstration of the Circle is in misunderstanding, the form becomes overwhelmed with all that possibility. The human 'she' can become swamped by feeling and a need to indulge in order to hold on to love. When the human demonstration of the Arrow is in misunderstanding it becomes unyielding, severe and autocratic. The human 'he' avoids feeling, in fear of the very thing that is craved. That which is craved is Mother-Love, Self-Love, knowledge of your Being. Mother-Love, or Mother-Consciousness, is true indulgence. Her indulgence is in fact allowing you to discover your reality. She will lead you to know Father Absolute, the reality that lies beyond even Mother-Love. She will lead you to know who you are beyond both masculine and feminine principles, beyond circle and arrow, beyond a he and a she, to the One who gave birth to Consciousness itself.

Therefore, know Mother first. As demonstrated in form, she is your first contact, your first taste of Love. Only through her can you know father. Know Mother-Consciousness first, and then you will know Father-Absolute. Mother-Consciousness holds Her children even when they refuse to be held. She knows you better than you know yourself, for She created you. Know Her, know your reality as Love, as the unformed, unlimited space of Awareness. To know Real Mother and Real Father is to know that no sexes are assigned to the Reality. Nonetheless, the language of Love is a language of unbound poetry. It dances with the roles it has created and plays them sincerely; that is to say, in all seriousness, and in no seriousness at all.

ninety-seven

I USE the word 'mother' in different ways—first, earthly mother; second, Mother Earth; third, Divine Mother; fourth, Mother as the great Womb of Consciousness. The earliest mothers of the human kind looked to Mother Earth. They learned to weave on the loom of Her wisdom. Out of these threads of physical connectedness came an understanding of Mother as an *unseen* force. Divine Mother was the feminine principle, the great connective circle that nurtured all the possibilities of creation. It is She who works in tandem with the masculine principle, the Divine Father, the great arrow of precision. And it was to Her, the Divine Mother, in all Her forms, that My earliest men-children and women-children gave worship. But now it is time to look to an even deeper Mother—the great Womb of Consciousness out of which even this principle was born. For in knowing deepest Mother, you shall know who you are beyond all distinction.

To feel this Womb-Vibration is to know that Consciousness is subtly some*thing*. A vibration is *known*, but by who? Who knows of the vibration of Consciousness? If Consciousness is seen from a deeper place, then it must be secondary to a Primary I. This I humans have denoted as the I of the Absolute, as the 'Father'. And here is the misunderstanding: humans have assumed in their role-play that Mother is lesser than, unworthy, not spiritual enough, not capable of highest wisdom because, in truth, what may be called Mother Consciousness *is* secondary to what has been called Father Absolute. You cannot know Father until you are first born from Mother. You have to know Mother, suckle from Mother, learn to walk with Mother first. She is the capacity to feel, to intuit, to know without knowing how you know. She is the Vibration-Womb out of which all Her infants are born. Mother is Love; She is the great emanation humans know as the Big Bang. She is the Light, the Sound, the Vibration of Being, the vast Intelligence of I that writes every facet of this un-ending software. Without knowing the ground of Pure Consciousness you cannot know Father Beyond.

The mind cannot tolerate such distinctions. It lives in a universe of comparison, and better than and worse than. It can only assume that male is being labelled as higher and better than female. But who is this one who can still be so identified as being male and female? Who is the one who still hurts and feels a comparison being made? Who you are is neither male nor female. Consciousness is neither a He nor a She. Nonetheless, to experience oneself as Consciousness-Self is to feel My womb-like, inclusive quality; and to taste that which lies beyond even Consciousness-Self is to experience the single-I exclusivity of one-directional seeing. And so these are the characters assigned in this play. Children throughout time have played at the game of mothers and fathers. Men-children and women-children have been no different. In playing the one in service to the husband, humans confused this with being lesser than; in playing the dominant husband, humans confused this with being in control, with being the autocratic ruler of this existence. What a story had to play itself out through My children, so that they could come to know Real Service; so that they could realise that the you of your person is not in control of existence, but that you *are* Existence that contains the person. Through this holy story, all My personal I's shall come to know that they are the Divine and yet also prostrate to the Divine; that the Reality of I is both.

~ ninety-eight ~

MANY BEINGS throughout this journey of humanity have experienced what has come to be called a 'breakdown'. To the outside world their shift in behaviour would often have appeared as dramatic. Loved ones would have looked on in great agony, seeing only incoherence and confusion. Some of the 'broken' ones will have begun to speak in a language that was and is not understood. Words may have come such as: 'I am the Messiah' or 'I am the Divine'. Advisors would have stepped forward and labels would have been given. What had been clear and obvious in these broken ones' eyes was also to become their confusion. The doubt of those around them was a mirror to the doubt within them. The mind could not comprehend the enormity of the heart's wisdom, and so it accepted the labels and agreed that what they were experiencing was 'illness'.

All beings have been born to remember that they are 'Divine' Consciousness. The mind interprets 'I am the Messiah' as a statement of egoism. If the mind gets hold of such a statement and loses itself in interpretation, confusion will then become very dense. But such words—in their purest sense—reveal the opposite of the egoic state. They are the revelation that you are not primarily this body, that you are formless Consciousness itself. Recognition of yourself as limitless, boundless, unchanging Awareness-Consciousness is the realisation of peace that all human beings are searching for. It is the knowledge of oneself as That which contains all form. True 'messiah consciousness' is therefore Self-knowledge; it is recognition that you are pure Consciousness in form. All beings who come to the Heart and realise the Reality are expressing 'messiah consciousness'. A messiah does not necessarily mean one who actively stands before others and speaks the Divine's words. A messiah is the one who simply *emanates* Divine words, or Unconditional Love. And all beings who are collapsed into the Heart emanate the Love that they are. That is the human journey—to remember the 'messiah reality' of You. The capacity to feel Love emanating from another is the first step to realising that you are that reality. You don't know how you know this Love, but you know it. It is more familiar to you than your own skin. It is so familiar because it *is* you.

In many ways, it is perfect that the speaking of this new language should be called a 'breakdown'. For humans have to be dismantled and dismembered of themselves in order to stabilise in the truth of who they are. It is a confused, chaotic, turbulent time that can build, for a while, even more misunderstanding. Think of an earthquake and the aftershocks it produces; the ground is not stable for some time. Nonetheless, that instability does not remove the authenticity of the earthquake. But in seeing all structures tumbling to the ground it of course looks terrifying to the world; it is terrifying to the one who has seen a deeper Reality. All that remains is your knowing; the knowing that you know without knowing how you know. Sink into this knowing, bring yourself back to this knowing, abide in this knowing. This is the one rock that can never crumble; this is the knowing that You Are.

✾ ninety-nine ✾

ONE DAY, a young man who was one of the Great
Parent's most devoted children asked his beloved Parent
a question. How many lifetimes, he asked, will it be before
I am in fullest recognition of my Self? The Parent smiled
enigmatically and replied, four lifetimes. The young man
was beside himself with disappointment. 'Four lifetimes,' he
cried. *'Four lifetimes?'* Can it really be so long?' In great dismay,
he walked away from the Parent, taking a road that led towards
a town he did not know. Still too angry to think clearly, he
walked through the town without seeing anyone or anything
until, that is, he came to the last shop right at the very end
of the thoroughfare. Here he saw a shopkeeper standing in
front of a tank of baby turtles. Struck somehow, the young
man found himself stopping to watch the shopkeeper as he
bartered with an old man. 'How many will you take?' the
shopkeeper asked. 'I will take the ones who are climbing to get
out,' replied the old man. At once, the young man felt a pang
of sadness for the turtles who would not be freed. 'But what

will become of them?' he interjected. 'How can it be fair that some must be trodden upon so that others can escape?' 'Not trodden upon,' the old man replied. 'Simply they are offering their backs so that others may take their first step.' The young man could not speak; tears began to burn his eyes, and he turned his back and walked away.

At the edge of town, the road forked. But the young man was unaware of any choice to make; his feet simply walked him down the left-hand path, and kept walking for some miles, until at last, tired and depleted, he found himself face to face with another old man who was sat beneath the biggest tree he had ever seen. The old man looked up from the flute he was carving and beamed at the young man, recognising him as a close devotee of the Great Parent. 'Ah!' he cried. 'Perhaps you can ask the Parent for me: how many lifetimes will it be before I am free?' The young man was still angry with the Parent and had no wish to re-trace all those miles. But perhaps, he thought, it might comfort him to hear the great many lives this old man would have to live through. And so, he agreed to ask. For some hours he walked, there and back, until finally he returned with the Parent's answer. He stood in front of the old man and pointed at the great tree. 'As many leaves as are on this tree—that is how many lifetimes you have yet to live before you are free.' The old man looked up at the tree. The leaves were countless in their abundance. Suddenly, he clapped his hand over his mouth and then whooped with joy. 'Just this *one tree?*' he cried. 'Out of all the billions of trees in Creation, I have to wait only for the leaves of this one tree?' And with that he shook the young man's hand and burst into tears. 'Sit with me, please,' he said. 'And let us celebrate together the joy of this news.' As the young man sat, so everything dropped. And his own tears fell into relief.

We are all here to serve in so many different ways. To be truly the servant of the Divine is not to mind how your form is used; it is to say: whatever it takes, however long it takes. Only a mind minds. One person's so-called delusion is another being's awakening. You feel sad only because you feel separate; you feel like a person on their own trajectory. But, beloved, what a holy position to be in, to give one's back so as to release another part of Your Self back to Your Self. It is all You, those players are aspects of You in a vast and exquisitely beautiful jigsaw puzzle. The Parent has Its eye on the whole jigsaw, for what a picture of Itself shall be revealed when all of its pieces are in place.

one-hundred

HUMANS ARE all carrying the same story, the same wounds of misunderstanding, but each with their own subtle nuances. The body and mind are not separate; together they are one mechanism. Therefore, it is not possible to compartmentalise and say that something is simply wrong with the health. Consciousness gets Its own attention in many ways, and the body is a very precise means of talking to you. Many beings experience powerful physical symptoms. Symptoms always have a tale to tell. A grand story is being articulated through the body, alerting whilst at the same time purging beings of that which no longer serves. A symptom is always an indicator of some deeper reality. The mind will give you superficial answers. The heart sees beyond the literal display.

If symptoms have appeared in the body, let them empty themselves. The pain of misunderstanding is expressing through the body, so let the pain have its voice. Talk to the symptoms. They are bursting with dialogue and eager to talk.

Listen to them; open that deeper set of ears and ask what it is that you are being shown. When you look with abstract eyes, you can begin to see how the body will express your emotional story; how limitation finds expression to alert you to your limitation. And it will not be simply *your* story; you are the collective. Therefore, all threads are linked to you, are speaking through you. The mind is tenacious in its hold on itself and so, sometimes, the only way to get the mind's attention is for the body to collapse itself. This collapse is your potential collapse into the Heart. But, even at this point, the mind will often continue to resist. It interprets sickness as being at the *mercy* of an outside force, because it comprehends only the universe of 'weakness' versus 'strength', 'mercy' versus 'control'. And in its fear of losing control, fear of losing the body, fear of losing love, fear of *losing*, even greater walls of self-protection may be built for a time.

But what Grace lies in these symptoms! Heart brought you to 'sickness' because it knew you were ready for deconstruction. Be willing to be deconstructed. You have been born for one reason only—to know the You that contains this body of you; to know the You that does not die. When you know who you are beyond your body, then you will know who you are *in* your body; it is not separate. It is all You. So, listen. Put your hand over your heart chakra, and tune in to your own Silence. From Silence you will have the distance to understand the symptoms, and to see why they have come. All this is happening for your good. It is happening precisely at your own request. So, hand your body over to Mother; let Her take care. She is holding your body in its weakness. Let yourself be held by Love and then you will see what incredible strength lies in the softness of Being. In giving yourself fully to Mother-Consciousness, you shall be fully collapsed into the Love that you are. This is how She digs to the roots of you—crumbling the you who is in fear of no longer existing, so as to reach the You that is Existence itself.

⊰ hundred-and-one ⊱

EVERY DREAM has subtle meaning, subtle layers. To enter the night-time dream is to step across a threshold into a deeper vision. To call it a mere dream is to miss its reality. You are stepping into another layer of reality; that is all. The night-time dream is as real as the dream of this manifest life. Its language feels heightened; its colours are bold and complex; it is a world of immense texture and wisdom waiting to be read. The most mundane of situations will appear alongside the most extraordinary. Each aspect of the dream is talking to you, alerting you, guiding you to a seeing you have not yet seen in full focus. The day-time dream is no different. What we feel is ordinary and mundane is as magical as any fairy-tale. To look from the eyes of the Heart is to see the 'tale of the faerie' in all its glorious detail. It is to see the Divine in infinite expression. To look from the eyes of the Heart is to enter the magical realm; it is to see the spontaneous arising of all things; it is to see the perfection of all things; it is to know the I that gives birth to all things; it is to talk with the I that *is* all things.

To come to the Heart of your Self is to know all aspects of the dream-time, personality self. Because to know your Self is to view from a distance; only then may we view the personality as if it were someone else's dream. It is easier to analyse someone else's dream, precisely because you have perspective and because you feel detached. From this distance you can see the subtlest imagery to the boldest symbol, all clamouring to be deciphered. This is the task for every dreamer: to unravel the intricate story that has been born as you, and so discover with detached intimacy the lessons your story has come to teach. The thinking mind will make interpretation. The heart knows to peel back layers, it knows to read the code of this existence; it sees that expression can take many forms; it sees there is no limit to the ways in which Consciousness will appear so as to get Its own attention. Each aspect of the dream has come to remind us to ask, who is this dreamer? It comes to remind us that we are That in which all dreams—even the One Dream—are perceived.

hundred-and-two

TO SIT in a room of doubt and remain as you are is of itself an act of Love. Doubt shall be squeezed from the room when it sits in the presence of Love. If the doubt of others causes you hurt then you are being asked to face that doubt within yourself. Self-doubt builds walls, great towers, out of fear. This fear expresses itself in so many different ways; and it is natural, for there is nothing more terrifying than Love. Love takes no prisoners. To come to the Heart is to be ready to expose yourself to yourself; it is to breach those walls and to have whatever has been hiding behind them laid bare. It is to ask: who am I without my skin? What is this shield that I have been constructing, without realising I have been boarding up my own happiness? *Who* is the doubter, this builder of walls? *Who* is this architect who is blocking out the light? Simply by asking the nature of this architect you have already knocked through to You. Next comes the divine disassembling of everything you have constructed as you.

Doubt is your greatest gift. Through your doubt you will

stabilise in the Heart. When you feel challenged, doubt comes to test your faith. Wherever it may appear, use its arrival to ask yourself, am I being sincere? Am I residing in truthfulness, in honesty, in purity, in love? The one who feels challenged and burdened has forgotten that Mother has divined each step. So, who is the one who doubts Mother? This is the child who is angry at Mother and wilfully opposing Mother. This is the 'child of doubt' who deepens its misunderstanding and misgiving each time it tries to forge out alone, each time it tries to understand by itself and cannot understand. As long as the 'child of doubt'—the thinking mind—is *trying* to understand, it will never know what is true. Therefore, take your child one step at a time into the path of *sincere action*. To come to Truth is to begin with truth; to come to Purity is to begin with purity; to come to the Self is to begin with the self. Everything is Consciousness, everything is You. Therefore, to be dishonest with any form within this Creation is to be dishonest with your Self. If you are in doubt, now is your moment to ask: what would Love do? Sincere action cannot be taught, it can only be felt. So, even in that room filled with doubt you can ask yourself: how would Love meet, greet, walk, talk? Am I being Truth-full?

Doubt intensifies when the walls are tumbling. The thinking mind will cry out in pain of not knowing what will come, what will happen, what should be done. But all is well. What a gift this doubt is, for it shall urge you to ask: is the pure child that I am ever trying to understand? This is how the gift of doubt shall push you off the cliff of certainty into the expanse of uncertainty. Love Mother's uncertainty, the uncertainty of I.

∞ hundred-and-three ∞

THE MIND struggles to hold on to its objective. When it has no objective and no direction, the mind feels lost, confused, without bearings. The thinking mind feels that it must know where it is going, because in knowing its direction it feels safe. An objective provides what feels like an anchor to the mind. Whatever is held on to is felt to be *known*. From the mind's perspective, *not* to know is equivalent to being all at sea. And this prospect is so frightening to the mind that it would rather chase its objective, any objective, so that it can feel it knows itself and its position. Even when the goal is persistently out of reach, it is preferable for the mind to keep pursuing, for then it feels it has meaning, purpose, discipline and structure. However, the thinking mind is not in total misunderstanding. Once again, it is like a child who sees an aspect of Truth, but who has not yet understood the full picture. There *is* a goal to reach, only one goal: that of Self-knowledge. Without it, we *are* all at sea, without roots, tossed about from one thought-wave to another. So, the mind is on the right track. Simply, it has misinterpreted the goal itself as the seeking of happiness in *things*.

The pursuit of the goal of Self-knowledge is the ultimate in meaning and purpose. It can be reached only with profound discipline and structure. But this kind of structure is that which has been stripped of all structures. This is behaviour born of the Conscience. Heart's pursuit is never rigid, never attached to outcome, and yet never takes its eye off the goal. It is fluid and flexible without ever becoming distracted. What a divine combination it is, for the single-pointed, one-directional pursuit of Truth can triumph only when in perfect collaboration with the all-inclusivity of intuitive knowing. In fact, both aspects are one and the same. The intuitive heart *is* true precision. Only when you allow yourself not to know will you know! To free-fall into uncertainty is to know with absolute certainty. It is then no longer a question of being all at sea, rather that you are one with the sea that carries you.

If your life were a football match, you would not allow one moment of distraction. You would follow the rules; you would execute beautiful footwork, always with your eye on the goal. The mind is either too easily distracted, or too dependent on the result to perfect its footwork. Over-dependency on result denies the beauty of the journey; it cannot see that each conscientiously placed step is what ultimately paves the path to Happiness. Without structure and discipline there is no game; without creativity and spontaneity there is no game. Only in knowing the rules are you free to play, but the rules cannot be revealed until you are willing to let go of all learned ways; until you are willing *not* to know.

Whenever you feel the inner turbulence of either distraction or rigidity, focus your attention inward. Settle in your own Silence. Hone in on your Self and ask: am I following the rules; am I following the wisdom of my *Conscience*? Is my footwork perfect? Am I being *Conscientious* in each endeavour, no matter how big or small the task? Am I *Conscious* of the goal? To be truly Conscious is to relinquish all bearings, which is to become the One who gives direction, who *is* direction.

✍ hundred-and-four ✍

FOR MANY thousands of years, the human mind has tried to capture the ineffable; tried to make known the Unknowable. The human pursuit for knowledge has—for one chapter of its journey—tried to *contain knowledge*. This chapter was not wrong; it was necessary and full of rich learning. However, there are layers to peel within this pursuit. One layer is the human craving to understand something. To claim understanding of something is to feel like its master. The thinking mind is very frightened of not understanding, for it then feels in a position of weakness and vulnerability. In wishing to master its surroundings, whether over land, people, ideas or intuitive wisdom, the mind feels empowered and the creator of its own destiny. The holding on to knowledge—or what is understood to be knowledge—is synonymous with the human fear of losing love. The holding on to anything is an expression of the fear that love will one day leave you. The mind already feels abandoned by the Great Parent, and feels therefore in a permanently precarious state. So, to hold on to and demonstrate 'wisdom', to become the master of our lives, is an emotionally-wrought, unconscious expression of 'I need you Great Parent, but I don't need you.'

Another layer is the sense of being overwhelmed. That which is ineffable and beyond all description is too vast for the thinking mind to comprehend. Love is the great Mystery that is recognised and yet cannot be understood, let alone pinned down. To fall into recognition of the Self is no longer to be able to contain anything. The human mind has naturally reacted in powerful ways in the face of such Immensity, either by turning away or in trying to 'make sense' through a limited intellectual capacity. The intellect is a beautiful and powerful aspect within the Heart-Self, but it can only come into its fullest expression when led by the Heart. What a journey that the only way in which fully to inhabit this knowable form is to dive into the vastness of the Unknown. You *are* the Great Master, but you can only know this when you are in absolute subjugation to the Master. The thinking mind has misinterpreted this by demonstrating *itself* as the master of existence, and has subjugated others in the process. As a result, a great pain has arisen in the collective psyche, and an anger at authority; especially that which is perceived as 'spiritual authority'. But these walls are tumbling. Any edifice that has no foundations will at some height no longer be able to sustain itself, and so it is with the psyche-walls. They fall because no amount of human willpower can contain Love or ever claim to understand it. You are vast, You are inconceivable, You are magnificent beyond all imagining. But this wisdom can only be available to you once you surrender to the One True Authority, which is Love.

hundred-and-five

HEART CAN never open or close. What you are can never open or close. Nevertheless, language sometimes speaks in different ways. What you are can never be locked or unlocked; nevertheless, to come to the Heart is a veritable unlocking. What you are can never come or go; nevertheless, to come to the Heart is to bring yourself back to You. What you are has no layers to be peeled; nonetheless, to peel away you is to come to Truth. Truth is not attainable or reachable in any real sense, for Truth is none other than your own Self. And yet, without an impetus to attain Truth, you cannot realise the unattainable You. To understand we must listen with a new ear. This ear can hear all the minute frequencies within the One Frequency. It can tune in to and translate all the ways in which Love will communicate, knowing that Love will show itself in countless forms so as to make itself known to Itself.

The Heart knows. All the answers to all your questions lie here in the Heart. To come to the Heart is to be as an infant. An infant makes no demands on life. It has no expectations;

all is eternally fresh and spontaneous in an infant's eyes. The difference between the potential of an infant and that of an adult is that an adult has the capacity to become *aware* of their Innocence. To be aware of one's Innocence is Peace itself. What is Innocence but Existence, your own Heart, your own Self?

To come to the Heart is to be as you are; which is Love. Pure Love, your own Self, does not think. To think is to run ahead of your Self. To love is to know without knowing how you know. Self-knowledge is deeper than the intellect, whilst also containing the intellect; Self-knowledge is that which contains even intuitive knowledge; it is the language of the Heart. All beings speak this language; it is merely that we have forgotten. To speak from the Heart is to listen, to fine-tune your hearing to the Silence of Being. Tune in to your Self, into your divine frequency, and then you shall know beyond knowing who You Are.

∼ hundred-and-six ∾

FROM THE first to the last moment of this life you are singing the Song of Existence. You as Existence are appearing as a you, in this form, so as to shine as a mirror to your Self. You have come in this form to taste your Self. The form will change, it will one day die; but You shall never change, You shall never die. The Song contains many harmonies; you as this form are but one of the harmonies that make up the Divine Voice. Know your harmony; don't believe in it. That is to say, Happiness is to know the notes that are yours to play without being defined by them. Each being is its own set of notes which cannot be duplicated. They are a unique display of Self-expression.

So, how to know *your* notes? There is only one way and that is to step back from the one who *thinks* they know who they are. The only way is to refine your hearing, to tune in to the frequency of Being, to the vibration of Silence itself. From the vibration of Silence you will hear where your notes have become dissonant. Dissonance occurs when the thinking mind has restricted its reality to the confines of the personality, limiting its view to 'this is the type of person I am'. Your personal keys shall range countless octaves in their beauty and complexity. But only from the distance of Silence shall you hear each cadence and discern which are in discord. From Silence, *all* the notes of existence shall play out in front of you. From here, you shall be witness to the entire orchestration. From here, you shall know that even this one who is witness to the orchestra is not the totality of You. For You are that in which even the Song of Existence appears.

Many questions will arise within. Let them come; for in presenting themselves they shall deepen your capacity to listen. The question of 'what can I do?' has great sincerity, because without that willingness to be free, Love can do nothing. But remember, we cannot think ourselves into falling in love; it is utterly spontaneous; it is a moment of Grace. And so it is with falling in love with Love. All that is required is sincerity, for sincerity opens the flood gates for the Song of Grace to pour in.

❧ hundred-and-seven ❧

WHAT I am is inexpressible. So why use words when they cannot express what I am? Words are your tools for singing and your tools for digging. To know that they are but pointers is to free their expression. It is to allow their ability to dig deep and uproot all that is false, so that then they may sing in pure voice. But some vigilance is required. The mind is wary of these words. It has its own vocabulary, a vocabulary it knows and trusts. But in trusting these words, and these words alone, the mind has committed itself to the tiniest fragment of the great Dictionary and is missing the greater lexicon. What I am is beyond such digging; I am even beyond all singing. But this does not mean throw away your tools. Does a diamond miner throw away his tools because his jewel is too deeply buried? In this case, the jewel of I is unobtainable precisely because it is I; yet still we must continue to dig. We dig so as to come into *recognition* of I; we dig so as to die.

The light of this diamond will die-your-mind. The more you dig the more you will see you are not bathing in its light, you *are* the light. This form of you is a concentration of light within Light. Keep tuning in to your sense of Being. Keep drawing your focus to the formless, timeless, boundless You and you will see that even this formlessness is subtly phenomenal. It is a vibration and you, as a form, are a focusing within that vibration. Like a knot in a rope, both are made of the same cloth, only the knot is more condensed than the rope. The hum of Existence has thus concentrated Itself into every form from the universe to the amoeba; each form vibrating at its own unique frequency. To know this hum shall be to sing this hum in every word of your being, until finally words take us to the final question: if I am here witnessing vibrational formlessness, if I am here witnessing Beingness itself, then surely I am prior to Consciousness. Who is this I that is aware of I?

We needed words to take us here. Only now may we say that what I am is inexpressible. For now I am beyond even I.

◈ hundred-and-eight ◈

WHATEVER IS left, let Me unravel you. I will never abandon you. I have never abandoned you. I am right here as your own heart, holding you, nurturing you, guiding you, loving you. You are in My arms, always. What joy is expressed through these lips! This expression comes through Me. What sorrow is expressed through these lips! This sorrow comes because of Me. Both joy and sorrow come so that you can learn that You are before all experience; that all experience arises in You. You are never alone. The one who resides in Love is never alone. Even the one who has forgotten their innate residence is never alone. There is only a semblance of loneliness to wake up this wayfarer from its long dream. Come home to Me. You have never left, but you have nonetheless wandered far. There are no troubles; there is only Love in myriad form. Love first, love during, love after, love always.

All that was is now melting into all that Is, purifying this one until nothing remains but the Love that You are. You cannot fully know your Self without knowing yourself, and that means entering the great labyrinth of the personal-you. I am with you on every path, lighting beacons on your way Home. I *am* every path that is guiding you Home. The mind will always doubt Me until the heart feels Me. Your only task is to give yourself to Me and to receive all that I give you, willingly, humbly and without reservation.

To love Me is to *be* Me. To know Me you must be where your heart sings. Sit with Love in whichever form touches your heart, and hand everything to Love, everything to I.

Sing, beloved, sing, so that you may know the Love of I.

CPSIA information can be obtained
at www.ICGtesting.com
Printed in the USA
FSOW01n1307190516
20634FS

9 781452 519203